MEDIEVAL SIEGE WARFARE

Text by
CHRISTOPHER GRAVETT
Colour plates by
RICHARD *and* CHRISTA HOOK

First published in Great Britain in 1990 by
Osprey Publishing, Elms Court, Chapel Way,
Botley, Oxford OX2 9LP, United Kingdom.
Email: osprey@osprey-publishing.co.uk

British Library Cataloguing in Publication Data
Gravett, Christopher
    Medieval siege warfare. – (Elite series; v. 28).
    1. Siege warfare, history
    I. Title   II. Series
    355.4409

ISBN 1–85532–947–6

Filmset in Great Britain
Printed through World Print Ltd, Hong Kong

FOR A CATALOGUE OF ALL BOOKS PUBLISHED BY
OSPREY MILITARY, AUTOMOTIVE AND AVIATION
PLEASE WRITE TO:

The Marketing Manager, Osprey Direct USA,
P.O. Box 130, Sterling Hts, MI 48311-0130
United States of America

The Marketing Manager, Osprey Direct UK,
PO Box 140, Wellingborough, Northants, NN8 4ZA,
United Kingdom

or visit Osprey's website at:
http://www.osprey-publishing.co.uk

Acknowledgements:
I should like to thank the following for their help in the
preparation of this book: Andrew Clary, Dominique
Collon, Sharon Johnson, Mark Murray-Flutter, Peter
Rea, Thom Richardson, Karen Watts and Barbara
Winter.

Dedication: For Jane.

Medieval Siege Warfare

Introduction

During the Middle Ages siege warfare played a vital rôle in military strategy. Sieges were far more numerous than pitched battles, ranging from small-scale affairs against palisaded earthworks to full-scale assaults on vast strongholds. Though a battle tends to be remembered, it was a dangerous gamble which could lead to the loss of large numbers of troops vital to a campaign. Prudent commanders were reluctant to throw caution to the winds unless there was good cause. When we turn to the castle, however, a different picture emerges. Castles controlled the countryside around them; they provided bases from which, particularly in the feudal era, squadrons of knights could ride out to attack an enemy. If an invader chose to bypass such a stronghold he left himself open to constant harrassment, and to a threat hanging over his lines of communication and supply. Further, castles were often situated on roads or rivers and frequently near junctions; therefore if an invading body was of inadequate strength it was forced to give such strongholds a wide berth, leading to major inconvenience and loss of time.

In order to secure a conquered country, the castles themselves had to be captured. One reason cited by the chroniclers for the relative ease with which Duke William subdued England after the Battle of Hastings was the lack of any system of castle-building in the country. Henry V won the French crown not by the morally uplifting but rather empty victory at Agincourt, but by the painstaking programme of sieges which followed. However, sieges were not only laid in order to win kingdoms, but also to subdue rebel vassals and robber knights. At other times belligerent lords used periods of weak rule to seize castles from their neighbours and fortify them against attempts at reclamation. A prime example is to be found in the brutal Robert of Bellême, who took several castles during the confusion on the borders of Normandy following the death of William the Conqueror in 1087. By contrast, in 15th-century Italy prudent generals of the bands of mercenaries called 'condottiere' might sit in front of a castle all summer, since a relief force of similar stipendiaries was usually loath to attack their entrenchments and risk all. It made for bloodless and profitable campaigns.

The science of siege warfare, or 'poliorcetics', was certainly not new to medieval man: the 'early' references occur in the Old Testament. Sieges are also vividly portrayed on Assyrian reliefs of *c*.900–600 BC, but the science was most fully developed by the Greeks and latterly by Roman military technicians. When the Roman Empire collapsed some of their skills were lost to the barbarian invaders who settled in Europe, but the writings of men such as Vegetius and Vitruvius were preserved and copied in monastic libraries; by the 12th century many religious houses con-

A representation of Jerusalem besieged, from 'Commentaries of Hayman on Ezekiel' of *c*.1000. The besiegers use wheeled battering rams and early forms of crossbow, and the stone buildings are surrounded by a wooden palisade. (Bibliothèque Nationale, Paris, Ms. Lat. 12302, f.1)

Norman knights use flaming torches to fire the palisades surrounding the motte at Dinan, from the Bayeux Tapestry. The summit supports a wooden tower whilst a flying bridge connects the motte to the bailey courtyard below (not shown here). The picture demonstrates the particular weakness of wooden defences. This use of fire can be seen in Carolingian illustrations made 250 years before the Tapestry. In this representation of a formal surrender the keys of the castle are transferred on the lances.

tained their works. The actual methods by which a castle could be taken did not show any major changes throughout the Middle Ages. The most notable differences were seen in the field of ballistics with the appearance of new siege machines and, ultimately, the development of gunpowder.

Castles and Fortified Towns

A castle was not just a fortress, it was also the residence of its lord. In this way it may be distinguished from the communal fortified burhs of the Anglo-Saxons and Carolingians, and from the purely military forts, such as those built by the Tudors along the south coast of England. Towns and cities, on the other hand, had often been fortified since their first appearance in history. With the establishment of castles the latter were often attached to a town, either to offer a final place of safety or, in a conquered land, to overawe the local populace.

The castle emerged as part of the feudalisation of Europe, possibly during the 9th century, as a symbol of lordship in a world witnessing the collapse of the Carolingian Empire and the incursions of Vikings, Magyars and Moslems. Though a capitulary issued in 864 by Charles the Bald, King of the West Franks, demands the demolition of illegally erected *castella* and *firmitates*, such evidence is rare until the following century. Perhaps the two earliest stone castles to survive are the towers at Doué-la-Fontaine (*c*.900) and Langeais (late 10th-early 11th century), both in northern France.

Two types of bore, here illustrated in a Byzantine treatise of the 11th century. By revolving the iron point of the bore (one of which ultilises a bow drill principle) a hole could be made in stonework. In practice both types would be protected under a stout wooden penthouse. (Vatican Library, Rome, Codex Grec. 1605, f.8v)

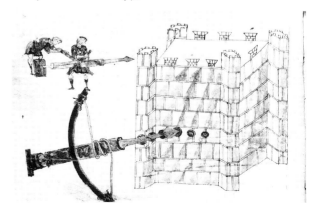

Doué-la-Fontaine began as a stone hall in about AD 900, and was converted 50 years later. A few other structures survive from this date, such as the border castles and watchtowers in the Roussillon in the Pyrenees. Some castles utilised disused Roman walls. Written evidence points to castles being built during the 10th century across Europe, but they were especially abundant in north-west France and Flanders, where feudal lordships were being formed, and which took the brunt of Viking attacks.

An early form of castle was the motte-and-bailey, often seen in France and Normandy in the 11th and 12th centuries and used to good effect by the Normans in England. This consisted of a mound (motte) of earth usually between 15 and 30 feet in height, sometimes revetted in timber, protected by a wet or dry ditch and surmounted around the summit by a palisade with a wallwalk. Inside this palisade stood a tall wooden tower, occasionally built on stilts to afford greater access. Below the motte was a courtyard or bailey, itself surrounded by a palisade and ditch and connected to the motte by a timber flying bridge, or a plank bridge and steps up the motte. Inside the bailey were the domestic quarters, stables, stores, forge and (most important) a well. Sometimes the mound was a natural hillock, while some castles simply consisted of a fortified enclosure, the so-called 'ring works'.

Although timber castles were cheap and quick to build, stone strongholds, with their advantages against fire, had been known from the beginning, and increased in number during this period. Similarly many castles were built using a mixture of stone and timber. Some mottes had their timber defences replaced by a stone wall with dwellings placed against its inner side. These structures are known as 'shell keeps'; that at Berkeley has the stone wall rising up from ground level to enclose the motte entirely. Few stone towers were placed on artificial mottes on account of their great weight, though some had their foundations at ground level with the motte of earth built up around them.

Many stone keeps were built during the 12th century in England and France, varying in size from 40 to 150 feet in length. They were usually square or rectangular, with a first-floor entrance

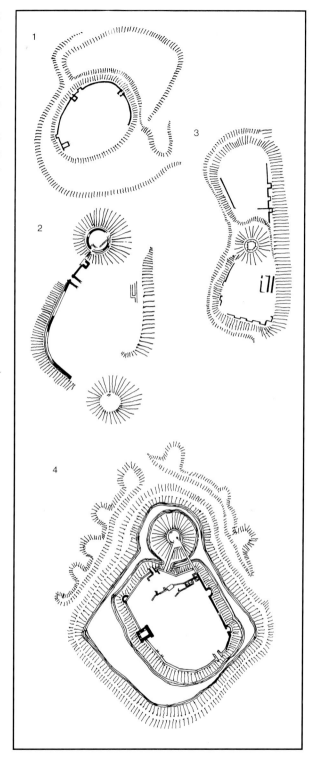

Earthwork castles of the 11th century.
(1) The ringwork at Saltwood, Kent, provided with a bailey. (2) Lewes, Sussex, with two mottes. (3) Windsor, Berks., with two baileys. (4) Berkhamsted, Herts., a motte-and-bailey whose ditch is often wet. The platforms beyond the ditches are probably those from the siege of 1216, when the castle surrendered to Louis of France after a bombardment lasting a fortnight.

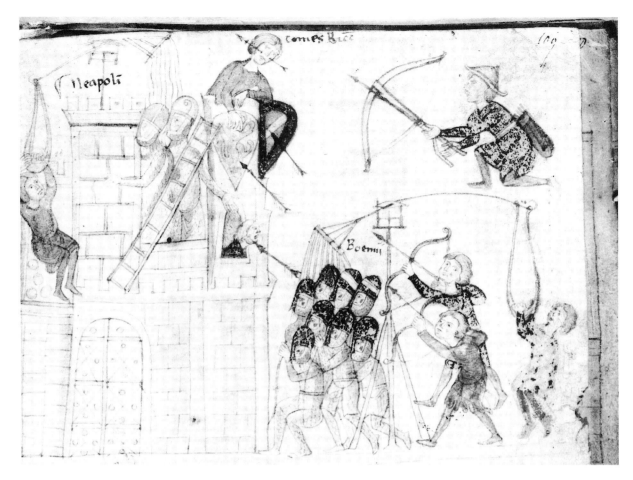

An early representation of a traction trebuchet from a Sicilian illustration dating to *c*.1180. By hauling on ropes the arm could be pulled down, causing the other end to fly up and release the missile. A man holds the sling to his chest to ensure it is in the right position for the launch, a characteristic of this type of trebuchet. A similar machine, used by the garrison, can be seen on the left. (Bibliothèque de la Bourgeoisie de Berne, Cod. 120 f.109)

often defended by a forebuilding, and a basement, living quarters and chapel contained on several floors, depending on the finances of the lord. Early versions (hall-keeps) tended to be squatter, with less floors than the later tower-keeps, in which the chapel might be contained in the forebuilding. A well was included, usually in the basement. The German equivalent was the *Bergfried*, a stone structure which acted as a watchtower but lacked the bulk of a keep. Many castles here were of earth and timber design. The keep was taken to the Mediterranean by the Norman conquerors of Sicily, and to the Holy Land by the Crusaders.

Occasionally keeps disposed of the rectangular plan. Thus the 12th-century keep at Orford in Suffolk is polygonal, whilst at Falaise in Nor-

mandy Philip Augustus erected a round tower next to the rectangular keep of Henry I. The latter design was an improvement on the angular variety; it left no sharp corners to offer a weak spot for the sapper's pick, and the gentle curve allowed a field of fire with none of the blind spots suffered at the corner of a rectangular building. Some round towers during the late 12th and early 13th centuries were drawn out on the side facing the enemy, rather like a ship's prow in shape. Towers with angles continued to be constructed throughout the Middle Ages, however.

In the 13th century, perhaps partly under the influence of Byzantine fortifications, castle builders began to put increasing emphasis on the strength of the curtain walls around the courtyard. Flanking towers jutted out beyond the wall, giving archers a field of fire along the face of the curtain. The keep fell out of favour; at Castel del Monte in Sicily Frederick II built an octagon, the outer angles covered with polygonal towers. Castles were often built with strong gatehouses and two

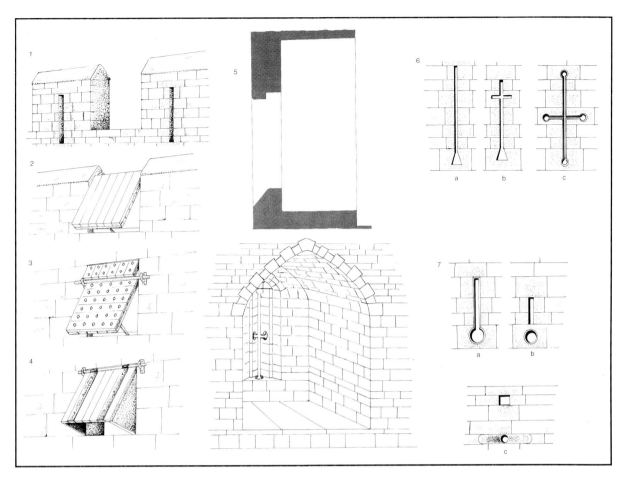

(1) Battlements were divided into 'crenels' or embrasures and 'merlons' or solid pieces. Here the merlons are provided with arrow-loops. (2) From the 13th century, wooden shutters provided added protection. A bar at the rear pivoted in a hole in one merlon and in a slot in the other, allowing the shutter to be dismantled. (3) and (4) Other forms of shutter. (5) An embrasure and sectional view; the loop is angled to allow defenders a wide field of fire while presenting a narrow frontal opening (see 6). (6) True arrow-loops were uncommon until the 13th century: (a) Late 12th century on. Note fish-tailed base to allow archers to shoot towards the foot of the wall. (b) Cruciform shapes were in use by the early 13th century. One chronicler states that the horizontal slit was specifically for crossbowmen. (c) Cruciform shapes with circular ends appeared as the 13th century progressed. (7) Loopholes to accommodate guns appeared at the end of the 14th century: (a) Early keyhole form. (b) Later medieval form with separate observation slit. (c) Late 15th century, with a wide splay externally.

concentric lines of walls, the inner usually higher to overlook the outer. Existing keeps might be similarly provided with defensive rings, as at the Tower of London. These concentric designs are seen throughout England, Wales, France and Spain. In Germany, where castles were frequently perched high on lofty crags, and where Carolingian palace architecture had influenced design for longer than in France, such strong walls were less in evidence and domestic ranges much more so. In the flat lands of the Low Countries *Wasserburgs* utilised large water moats as added protection.

During the 14th and 15th centuries there was little actual advance in castle architecture, save that a gradual alteration in social living standards tended to favour an emphasis on comfort rather than defence, reflected for example in the occasional recourse to square towers, more integrated domestic ranges, and larger window openings through external walls (except in Spain). Some areas, however, always found a need for castles with high security. France, ravaged by the Hundred Years War with its attendant misery of marauding English and Burgundian armies and troops of mercenary bandits, remained aware of the importance of strong castles, which posed more of a threat to their enemies than battle in the open field. In Spain the thrusting Christian chivalry threw up numerous castles in their *Reconquista*. Here especially, though also common in other

Rochester castle, Kent, a large keep and forebuilding built in Kentish rag by William of Corbeil in *c.* 1127. The single round corner turret bears witness to the siege of the barons by King John for almost two months in the autumn and winter of 1215, when royal miners breached the outer wall and drove a mine under the keep. Having filled the cavity with wooden props and pig fat, the whole was fired and the corner collapsed. Even then the defenders retreated behind the great cross wall, which divided the keep internally, and continued to resist. When rebuilt, the corner was given the present rounded face, which left no sharp corners for sappers.

parts of Europe, the keep reappeared, usually furnished with round towers and turrets. Small versions, such as the Scottish tower houses, were ideal in border warfare. In Germany the influence from the West was evident in the enlargement of some *Bergfried* to resemble keeps, as at Gutenfels. Moreover, some castles were built on lower ground, in which case they resembled their western counterparts rather than the often cramped hill strongholds. In the later Middle Ages the variety of castle designs increased to a bewildering extent. The idea of concentric castles fell from favour, defence relying more on a great curtain wall and towers; yet often the machicolated parapets and slim turrets suggest a desire for show rather than military practicality.

The Crusades

The incursions by the Christian West into the Moslem East provide two important topics for the study of siege warfare. The first is the sheer size of the structures encountered by the Latin armies as they crossed into first Byzantine and then Moslem territories. The great fortifications of Constantinople had been built originally by Theodosius II in 413, and presented three lines of walls, two sets of them with mural towers, with the river flowing in front. When the city was actually attacked by the men of the 4th Crusade in 1204, the Western soldiers assaulted the weaker sea wall from the Golden Horn, the landward fortifications remaining unassailed until the Turks finally took the city by storm in 1453.

The men of the 1st Crusade (1095–1099) soon found that even their full force, large for a Western army of the time, was unable to completely surround a great city such as Antioch, and had to contend with guarding principally against sorties from the several gates, for which they built their first fortification. The Crusaders soon began to build castles to assist their thrust against fortified towns. Thus Tyre was hounded by troops from the castles of Toron and Iskandaruna, 13 and nine miles respectively from the city, which fell in 1124. When Saladin came to prominence the crusader castles took on the role of border posts, offering safe havens, obstacles to invaders and garrisons which could retire to join the Frankish army forming up behind. As in the West, however, the castle was also a centre of lordship and administration, and encouraged Frankish settlers to colonise areas under its protection. This is shown in the way some Frankish rulers utilised earlier Byzantine or Moslem defences regardless of actual frontiers; moreover, not all castles were set along borders vulnerable to enemy attack, some routes being relatively poorly supplied with strongholds.

The main theme in Crusader defences was the utilisation of natural defences. The crusaders themselves discovered an extreme example when in 1182 the defenders of the cave fortress at el-

Habis had to be dug out by the Latin forces. Often use was made of a spur of land protected on three sides by water, such as 'Atlit on the coast, or Sahyun at a river junction in the Syrian mountains. In such cases the vulnerable fourth side was protected by a ditch and here also stood the strongest walls. Where a rocky scarp could be used, castles such as Kerak in Moab were built to fit the contours, and so 'wards' or courtyards were not set inside one another in a concentric ideal. Many other crusader castles in Syria (such as Safita) bear the stamp of the Western keep, though less ornamented, with fewer loopholes, and with a ground-floor entrance. Because of a shortage of wood they were often internally vaulted, giving a squat appearance but making them more impervious to fire and providing a flat roof for a large fighting platform. Keeps were sometimes enclosed within tight curtain walls provided with vaulted buildings inside them, so producing wide wallwalks, yet protecting the base of the keep by their very proximity to it.

The castles that perhaps have raised the most interest are those which suggest the influence of Byzantine ideas which then crossed to Europe. The great majority of such castles consist of a square or rectangular enclosure provided with towers at the corners and at intervals along the curtain wall, rather in the nature of a Roman *castrum*. Such structures tended to be built in areas lacking natural defences. Their very vulnerability necessitated constructing them as quickly as was practicable, hence the shape. However, Byzantine ideas were known from late Roman military writers such as Vegetius, whilst Roman works (Portchester, for example) still survived in the West. Some castles, such as Ludlow, had stone curtain walls without a keep before the time of the 1st Crusade. Moreover, when the crusaders adapted a Byzantine fortress their walls might be placed adjacent to the older work rather than in an inner ring. Byzantine ideas included the isolation of each section of curtain by a mural tower with no access from the rampart, and casemates set in the curtain and provided with arrow loops to give a second line of fire, both styles which did not become general in the West. The use of an entrance in the side of a tower to expose the attacker to fire along a mural wall, and a second gate set at right angles, are also features in late Roman work. Latterly concentric defences might be added, as they had been in the West.

The castle at war

When war threatened the prudent castellan busied himself in making ready for any eventuality. When Bishop Odo of Bayeux rebelled against his brother William I in 1088 his supporters dug fortifications, strengthened their garrisons and laid in provisions. Often ditches needed clearing out and sometimes re-cutting, or crumbling masonry required repair. Any trees in the immediate vicinity would be cut down so as to deny cover to the enemy, a fate which might also befall any villages nestling close to the castle, to deny food or wood to a besieger. Wooden hoardings or 'brattices' were built atop the battlements to jut out and command the wall base.

The gate was the most vulnerable part of a castle, and this was always the site for some additional defensive measures. At first the gate might be protected by placing it within a timber tower, and in some 12th-century castles (Richmond in Yorkshire, for example) the entrance was guarded by placing it within a keep-like tower. This was not wholly satisfactory, however, and

The severed heads of enemy soldiers are lobbed into a fortress by catapult to demoralise the defenders. Such brutality was especially common during the crusades. This French illustration dates to the first half of the 13th century. Occasionally rejected letters were nailed to the severed head of a messenger and shot back. (Bibliothèque Nationale, Paris, Ms. Français 2630 f.22v)

9

Wooden hoardings or 'brattices' were built out from a wall to allow offensive materials to be dropped through gaps in the floor. They might have tiles or raw hides on the roofs. (1) A hoarding erected on a flat-topped wall. (2) Beams inserted through holes below the battlements support the hoarding. (3) The use of stone corbels to support the timbers at the keep of Coucy in France. (4) Stone machicolations allow the battlements themselves to overhang the wall base.

most castles adopted the idea of placing two mural towers close together, with the gate itself between the two. From this simple design arose the great gatehouses which can still be seen. They presented to the attacker a series of obstacles which he must pass to gain entry to the courtyard.

The first was usually the ditch or moat of the castle, crossed by a lifting bridge leading to the gatehouse. Beyond the bridge might be a series of solid doors secured by drawbars either running into slots in the masonry (these can often be seen) or revolving on a central pivot. Often a portcullis, a lattice of wooden beams shod with iron, was dropped along grooves in the wall to bar the way. Above the gate passage were holes in the vault or ceiling—*meurtrières*—through which offensive materials could be dropped. At Caernarvon the King's Gate was fitted with two drawbridges, six portcullises, and five doors, together with loopholes and a right-angled turn. Gatehouses were sometimes protected by an outwork—the barbican—in which two parallel walls guarded the castle gate and were often themselves given a gatehouse, thus allowing the adjacent walls to be enfiladed by fire. Occasionally earthworks and small towers were employed. Sometimes manuscript miniatures show an iron grille which could pivot up to allow a passage beneath when no danger threatened.

Other refinements were added to the defences; a

Types of drawbridge in use. The earliest castles might have a wooden bridge which was simply rolled back. A smaller gate and bridge were occasionally built beside the main one.
(1) The lifting bridge, using a winch and chains to raise the platform. (2) The bascule bridge, where beams with counterpoise weights were used. Introduced in about 1300, this method became popular in France and Italy. (3) A turning bridge, which pivoted in the middle; by withdrawing a bar from under the heavier inner side the front end pivoted up against the door whilst the inner side swung down. This type left pits both in front and behind. Notice the water shoot above the gate to help douse fires started by an attacker, and the 'meurtrières' or 'murder holes' in the passage ceiling which might have been for the same purpose or for dropping offensive materials through.

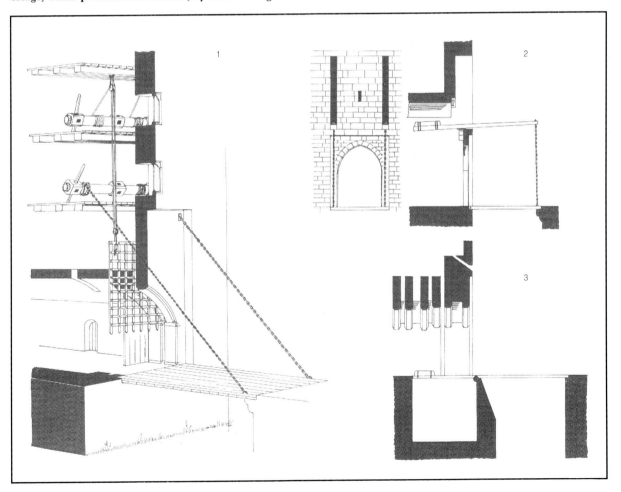

The old and the new; Falaise in Normandy. Henry I built the square keep and Philip II of France added the walls and round tower in the early 13th century. (Courtesy of the French Government Tourist Office)

talus or sloping plinth at the foot of walls added thickness against attempts to breach it, and allowed material dropped from above to bounce out against attackers. From about 1200 arrow slits were being provided in battlements, and loopholes and embrasures set in passages in the walls. For offensive counter-attack, sally ports or postern gates were built into castles to allow surprise attacks against the besiegers by mounted contingents. Some castle towers may have been specially built to take siege engines; in 1343 the Engine Tower at Criccieth is reported to have possessed its own springald.

Castle garrisons

Royalty and their higher nobility were the members of society who actually controlled castles, though in time of unrest lesser men might construct defences and hope to keep them after the disturbances settled down. If a lord was absent or dead the lady of the castle might resist an aggressor vigorously, as did Nicolaa de la Haye, widow of the sheriff of Lincoln, who held out against rebel forces in 1217. Powerful men had castles scattered over their lands, providing places of rest during a progress as well as security. In Spain the uncertain temper of life meant that castles were rarely used as fortified residences.

In the German Empire as late as the early 12th century the majority of nobles did not dwell in castles. However, the practice developed whereby castles were entrusted to unfree knights (*ministeriales*, peculiar to this area) or hereditary castellans. Some parts of France relied on hereditary castellans as in Germany, a practice which made the latter responsible to the lord or monarch for the upkeep of the castle. Elsewhere (except in Sicily, where castles had virtually no garrison in time of peace) and across the Channel in Anglo-Norman England garrisons were changed on a rota of castle-guard, whereby as part of their feudal duty soldiers spent a period of time garrisoning their lord's castles, a system which formed part of the same service as their 40 days service in the field. The length of service varied between castles, from as little as 15 days once or more per year to as much as four months in every 12; three months might be taken as average. Some were expected to discharge their duty only in time of war. In compensation for castle-guard release from wartime field service was sometimes allowed, though this was not always the case. Especially in France and Normandy the burden was left to sergeants.

Castle-guard was felt by some to be an onerous duty and was soon commuted to a money payment or *scutage* so that professional mercenaries could be hired. The chronicler Jocelin of Brakelond wrote that in 1196 the abbey of Bury St. Edmunds was expected to send 40 knights in constabularies of ten knights each to serve at Norwich castle, but actually the knights were debating whether to pay 2s. 5d. or 3s. to commute. In 1193 37s. 6d. was needed from the abbey knights to allow a force of 25 knights, 25 mounted sergeants and 25 foot sergeants to be hired. Not all knights wanted to send money; Magna Carta contains the provision that no one could be forced to pay if they preferred duty instead. Such scutage was popular with monarchs and great nobles, so that increasingly during the 13th century garrisons contained a percentage of hired troops. Household mercen-

aries might also travel with a great man and swell a garrison when he stayed at a particular castle. Even in the 15th century feudal troops were being used to garrison some castles in France.

It was in places such as Wales, the crusading areas of Spain, the Holy Land and the eastern frontier of the German Empire that fortresses were kept on an almost permanent war footing. The Holy Land was organised on a feudal basis. Mercenaries, including Turcopoles and Syrians, may sometimes have performed garrison duties. Many crusader fortresses were held by members of the military orders. The Templars garrisoned their castles with the knights and sergeants of the order, as well as mercenaries (Templars employed foot-soldiers apparently in companies of 50, 15 of which are recorded in the garrison of Le Chastellet).

Besiegers trapped between a relief force and a sortie by the garrison, from the Maciejowski Bible of *c.*1240. In the background a traction trebuchet is released, an artilleryman holding out the sling as it begins to rise. (Pierpont Morgan Library, M.638, f.23v)

Volunteers from Europe came to assist in the struggle. The Hospitallers also employed mercenaries to garrison castles, often infantry and Turcopoles. In 1212 they brought 2,000 and 1,000 men from the castles of Krak des Chevaliers and Marqab respectively in peacetime, whilst in 1271 Krak was held by 200 brother knights and sergeants. Yet castles in these areas suffered from shortages of men when they were needed in the field to oppose the enemy. In 1187 the master of the Knights Templar called out several garrisons to join in an attack on Moslem plunderers in Galilee; the chronicler Ernoul himself was sent to al-Fule, one of the castles involved, and found only two sick men left inside. Except perhaps for the period between the early establishment of the Latin East and its decline, it was extremely difficult to field an army and to garrison castles adequately. The Teutonic Knights, after their move to the frontiers of Germany when Acre fell in 1291, set up *Komturei* or commanderies in Prussia and Livonia, housing at least 12 knights and 100 brethren, mercenaries and militia, under a *Komtur* or a castellan, or a *Vogt* if isolated.

Town defence

Towns were usually defended by bands of militia. Philip Augustus recognised the value of the French

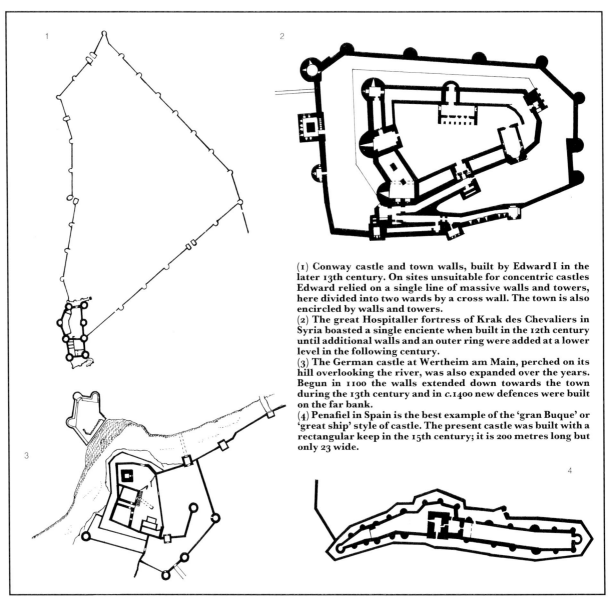

(1) **Conway castle and town walls, built by Edward I in the later 13th century. On sites unsuitable for concentric castles Edward relied on a single line of massive walls and towers, here divided into two wards by a cross wall. The town is also encircled by walls and towers.**
(2) **The great Hospitaller fortress of Krak des Chevaliers in Syria boasted a single enciente when built in the 12th century until additional walls and an outer ring were added at a lower level in the following century.**
(3) **The German castle at Wertheim am Main, perched on its hill overlooking the river, was also expanded over the years. Begun in 1100 the walls extended down towards the town during the 13th century and in *c.*1400 new defences were built on the far bank.**
(4) **Penafiel in Spain is the best example of the 'gran Buque' or 'great ship' style of castle. The present castle was built with a rectangular keep in the 15th century; it is 200 metres long but only 23 wide.**

The ruthless treatment of captured defenders, as shown in the 13th century Maciejowski Bible. Here a siege machine is adapted to hang the garrison commander. It may be a form of 'crow' for hooking up enemy soldiers. Meanwhile a sortie is routed. On the right one man saps the wall with a pick whilst another uses a scaling ladder. A number of the figures wear collars, probably of iron or bone covered by cloth. Many infantrymen have kettle hats, whose wide brims were ideal against materials dropped from above. (Pierpont Morgan Library, M.638, f.10,v)

communes, which had appeared in the second half of the 11th century, and used them as garrison troops. He especially confirmed the charters of frontier communes such as Picardy. In 1194 the *Prisée de Sergents* listed those sergeants expected from communes and abbeys of the royal demesne for three months in the year. During the 14th century some permanent contingents of crossbow-men, such as the *Corporation des Arbaletiers* in Paris, were raised for town defence. The 1448 Ordinance created the *francs-archers*, who served in exchange for a reduction in certain taxes and each of whom was maintained by a parish. (However, their conduct left something to be desired: when Charles the Bold of Burgundy arrived before Roye the town was defended by a few men-at-arms and 1,500 *francs-archers*, several of whom jumped the walls the next day and surrendered, to be followed by the rest next morning.) In those fortresses captured by the English during the Hundred Years War garrisons were maintained largely by indenture, that is by troops hired under a contract agreed between a nobleman and the king. In the 15th century they were annually drawn up and commissions of array were then issued quarterly for musters, pay being granted also quarterly, after the muster rolls had been checked. Rouen held 60 men-at-arms and 180 archers, smaller places con-siderably less. Calais and other important strong-

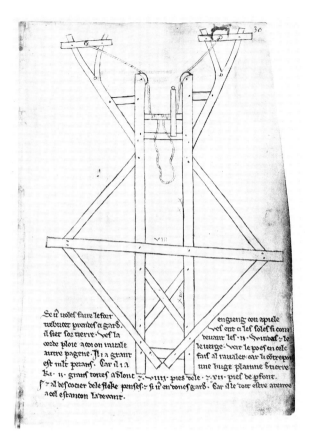

A sketch by Villard de Honnecourt made in about 1250 and showing the base plan of a trebuchet ground frame. The long arm carrying the sling would be at the top. The curved side pieces apparently acted as springs when wound on one of the windlasses; on release they would pull the arm bearing the sling down from the vertical sufficiently for the second windlass to come into play. Unfortunately any drawing of the side elevation has been lost. (Bibliothèque Nationale, Paris, Ms. Français 19.093, f. 30.

holds had large garrisons (1,000 at Calais). Many Frenchmen who found their lands ceded to England by the treaties of Brètigny and Troyes served loyally.

In England itself early town militias had looked after the walls; these bodies were sometimes well equipped, as at London, with helmets and mail shirts. The old Anglo-Saxon *Fyrd* service continued, though now as the obligation of all freemen to fight. Henry II's Assize of Arms in 1181 specifies padded *gambeson*, iron *capelet* (helmet) and spear as equipment. After the Norman Conquest household knights often stayed as garrisons in castles even after the country had settled down somewhat. Even a century later they were found in castles rather than settled on estates. The Lancastrians especially revived town militias during the Wars of

the Roses, mostly archers on foot, an increase from the 14th century, when towns had far fewer archers than the rural 'hundreds'.

In Spain all freemen of military age were expected to serve, though often beyond the town itself. Each town militia bore its own standard and was commanded by a *Juez*. Rich citizens who could afford horse and armour served as *Caballeros Villanos*. In the later 13th century an urban militia, the *Hermandad* or Holy Brotherhood, arose in Castile to guard itself against popular revolt or royal aggression; by 1315 one hundred cities had joined it. The Low Countries raised troops also based at first on brotherhoods, since the town guilds were an important element in society. By the late 13th century they were formed into constabularies of men from individual districts and streets of a city. Able-bodied men were equipped by their guild. Both fighting men and valets were provided. A *voud* was apparently a unit of 96 mounted burghers and 511 self-equipped guildsmen; in 1303 Bruges could muster 1,254 men.

In the German Empire towns were divided into quarters or *Vierteln* each under a *Viertelmeister*. The mayor usually led the militia, though mercenaries, hired increasingly to protect dangerous areas of the town and external suburbs, also gradually appeared as captains. The costs incurred often meant that municipal authorities could only produce small forces, though many towns boasted drill squares, and by the later 14th century a *Büchsenmeister* might be employed to organise artillery. Austria under the Habsburgs was able to field a force of cavalry (1000 in 1432) to guard the frontier, since the Diet argued less with the ruling princes than did those in the rest of the Empire.

Italy, with its classical tradition of town-dwelling, contained many houses with tall, fortified towers built by noblemen who lived in the urban environs. True vassalage was often supressed. Each town was also divided into quarters to provide a company of cavalry and infantry, though by the mid-12th century all who could served on horseback. All citizens of age for service were expected to come, though again they sometimes only manned the walls in time of danger. In the 14th and 15th centuries *provisionati*, consisting mostly of footsoldiers, were hired by the state for permanent garrison work, though by the second half of the 14th century they were also serving as bodyguards; Milan could boast 1,000 by the 1420s. By 1450 in both Milan and Venice selective militiamen were included, called out for emergency service under constables.

In the Holy Land towns supplied contingents of sergeants who probably served on foot. Italian communes also assisted where necessary in towns in which they had quarters. The military orders similarly held designated areas of some towns such as Acre.

Setting a Siege

Diplomacy

Setting a siege did not always entail risking the lives of soldiers, but it was still costly in time and money, since feudal troops might stay in the field beyond the limits of their service, and hired soldiers required payment. Hence, if a siege could be forestalled by diplomatic means this was beneficial to a commander. Thus William II allowed Stephen of Aumâle to fortify a castle on the Bresle in 1089 at the king's expense and to fill it with a royal garrison. William of Malmesbury remarked that such a method was more to the taste of Henry I.

Lords who were somewhat reticent could be encouraged by more forceful means, such as imprisonment. Thus when Empress Matilda captured Ralph of Esson in 1138 she refused to release him until he handed over his castles.

On occasion the reputation of a commander was such that his appearance in the field was enough to cause a stronghold to surrender without the need to resort to a lengthy siege. The fortification of Nonancourt and Illiers-l'Évêque and the possession of Sorel by Henry I in 1112 caused many potential troublemakers in the county of Maine to offer their fealty.

The formalities of siege warfare

If diplomacy failed to induce an enemy to yield up his strongholds it was necessary to appear in force

A representation of an assault using a crude siege tower, in a 13th-century Spanish manuscript. Wheeled up by knights below, the assault troops cover themselves with their shields as they close with the Moslem defenders. Notice the man on the tower wearing a coat of scale armour (Biblioteca Nacionale, Madrid, MS.195/Oronoz)

before the gates. When the code of chivalry was properly honoured the commander of a besieging force called upon the garrison to surrender before hostilities commenced. If this was accepted the recognised practice was to allow the occupants to march out unharmed, often with their arms and equipment. If the call was rejected, then a besieger was within his rights to sack the town and slaughter the inhabitants. This is graphically illustrated by the siege of Mequinenza in Spain by King Alphonso of Aragon in 1133. His invitation to leave with all possessions was rejected with scorn, but when an outwork fell three weeks later the castellans sued for peace and asked that their men be granted liberty. The angry king reminded them of their insult to Christ, stormed the castle and beheaded those he captured. The chroniclers note that when Jerusalem fell in 1099 it was neither sacked nor burned as was the custom in conquered cities, though a terrible bloodbath ensued. Towns and cities often suffered cruelly when captured. Henry I forbade plundering when Breteuil opened its gates in 1119 to allow him to besiege his wayward daughter in the citadel; yet that same year he put Êvreux to the torch when it refused to co-operate, paying compensation for the churches that were destroyed. During the civil wars of Stephen's reign Earl Ranulf of Chester was described as a barbarian for his sack of Lincoln in 1141. Even when a commander was disposed to mercy his soldiers might be carried away by their lusts. When Dover submitted to Duke William after the battle of Hastings some squires set fire to a number of houses despite his command that the town be spared—an act for which he gave ample reparation. At Exeter after a vigorous siege William actually posted guards at the gates to stop the rank and file (*gregarii milites*) from breaking in and plundering.

The members of a defeated garrison were more likely to be treated with leniency after a siege than

Angers castle, France. Largely built in the 13th century, a keep is no longer deemed necessary as part of the design. (Courtesy of the French Government Tourist Office)

A bow stave thought to be from a ballista, perhaps 13th century in date. The ends are provided with nocks for the string, and the arm is four feet long. The iron ballista bolt head is square in section and was found in the ruins of Gundisau castle, Zurich, destroyed in 1340. (By courtesy of the Board of Trustees, Royal Armouries)

the inhabitants of a town. This probably arose from the recognition that the soldiers were simply obeying the wishes of their lord in holding a fortress. Similarly prisoners captured by the garrison from a besieging army might receive good treatment, as happened in 1098 when William Rufus' garrison at Ballon seized men from the army of Fulk of Anjou. William later released them on parole, refusing to believe that a true knight would break his word. Honour was of great importance; thus the garrison in Vignats actually hoped to be stormed and thus allowed the opportunity for a dignified surrender to Robert of Normandy (1102).

The garrison commander was sometimes placed in a quandary when faced with a formidable enemy and with no clear instructions from his lord. Should he surrender immediately or risk death if his castle fell? Thus on occasion a castellan would formally ask permission to send to his lord before hostilities began, or even during hostilities, in order to ascertain what he was required to do. A time limit might be set, with the stipulation that unless relieved by a certain date the castle was to surrender. During this respite the besiegers might move on to another target, but the castle was still under siege. In 1102 the rebels in Arundel, after a three-month siege, were allowed to send to their lord, Robert of Bellême, to request reinforcements or leave to surrender. Powerless to help, Robert told them to yield. Henry I was angry when his own garrison of 140 hand-picked knights at La-Motte-Gautier-de-Clinchamp surrendered to Fulk of Anjou in 1118, but the garrison reminded him that their requests for help had been ignored. Mercenaries, too, expected to surrender with honour, as witness those inside Bridgnorth who had to be locked up when the garrison surrendered to Henry I in 1102, since they looked upon such an

act as a loss of honour. Not every garrison was treated humanely; a fit of anger could dispel notions of chivalry. Henry I razed Bayeux in 1105 after the castellan handed over a prisoner but refused to yield up the town. He and the garrison were subsequently seized. Similarly, a man once pardoned received short shrift if taken again in revolt.

When a castellan refused to surrender or to ask for truce, the besiegers might resort to other methods. Sometimes a threat was enough, as when William Rufus set up a gallows before Le Mans and threatened to hang knights, soldiers and townsmen each day; or when his brother, Henry I, threatened to hang everyone he could lay his hands on inside Bridgnorth castle if it did not surrender within three days. Captives were employed in the use of terror, as in 1139 when King Stephen captured Roger le Poer and threatened to hang him outside the gate unless his mother, who held Devizes castle, submitted. During the long siege of Antioch by the men of the 1st Crusade, Moslem prisoners brought back from Harenc in 1097 were solemnly beheaded by Count Bohemond's men, whilst the following year one hundred severed heads were also brought back to camp to encourage the crusaders and demoralize the enemy. The chronicler Froissart speaks of a messenger, captured during the siege of Auberoche in 1345, being placed in the sling of a trebuchet with his letters round his neck and shot back over the walls. Cruelty was not confined to the besiegers. When Sir Edmund Springhouse fell off a scaling ladder during Henry V's siege of Caen in 1417 the French threw burning straw on the knight as he lay in the ditch and roasted him in his armour.

Morale was of the greatest importance during a siege. Loss of morale could push the defenders to surrender, as happened at Bréval in 1092 when Robert of Bellême's siege engines broke the garrison's nerve. Besiegers too, could suffer. At Antioch several nobles fled by night after their attack on the Iron Bridge fortress had failed, whilst even after the city had fallen Bohemond had to light fires to drive his men from the houses to man the barrier against the hostile citadel.

A respected commander could urge his men to great deeds and demoralise the enemy. The presence of Joan of Arc in the siege lines at such strongholds as Jargeau, Meung and Beaugency caused swift surrender. By contrast the commander's fall could result in the collapse of morale. Richard Silvanus, a robber baron in the Avranchin who took advantage of the death of Henry I, was killed by Stephen's men during a raid. When his corpse was flung down before the

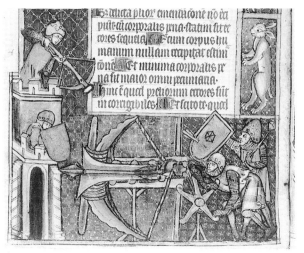

(1) **A ballista or giant catapult, from the manuscript of Walter de Milemete dated 1326. The powerful bow is tensioned by the windlass at right. The wheeled ballista (2) is from the 'Romance of Alexander' of c.1330, and is bent by a screw. Here the arms appear to be separate and may have been held taught by skeins of twisted rope as used in Greek and Roman versions as shown in the 11th-century Byzantine drawing (3). The 16th-century illustration by Lipsius (4) gives a better idea of the appearance of the latter machine. (Oxford, Christ Church Ms.92, f.68v and Bodley Ms.264 f.201r)**

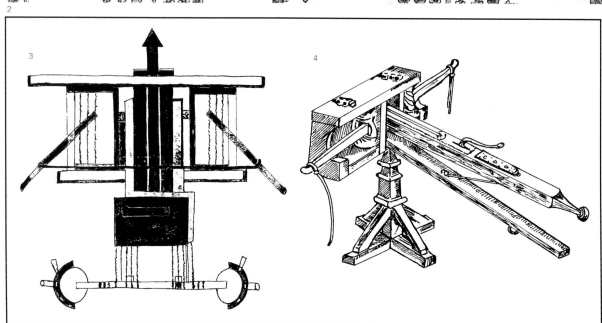

gate of his castle at Saint-Pois his men immediately surrendered. Similarly William Clito personally intervened to help his men besieging Aalst in summer 1128, so encouraging them that they defeated a relief column and beat back a sortie from the gates. When he died from an infected wound five days later his household concealed the news from the Flemings and foreigners in the army. In 1365 Louis Roubaut and his best soldiers were captured in an ambush, an act which led to the surrender to the Seneschal of Auvergne of the garrison of Brioude and several other strongholds. Morale was also boosted by the use of 'gallows humour'; when a stone killed the man standing next to William Rufus during the siege of Mayet in 1099 the garrison shouted that the king now had fresh meat. The siege castles in front of Gasny (probably erected in 1118) were given derisory names by the French defenders, 'Ill-placed' and 'Hare's form'. However, when the Scots departed from Wark in 1174, the garrison were ordered not to shout abuse in case they returned. Froissart remarks on the habit of defenders of pulling off their caps or taking cloths and ostentatiously dusting the masonry when it was struck by stones from catapults.

Laying a siege

Sieges were usually begun in spring or summer, during the campaigning season. Hot weather also assisted in the use of fire. It was less common to begin a siege during the winter, with its attendant difficulties such as freezing moats full to overflowing from winter rains. Some sieges, although begun

Marienburg, a stronghold of the Teutonic knights in Poland, begun in the 13th century and extended during the 14th before being lost to the Poles in 1457. It is typical of the Order's eastern strongholds, being built of brick near a river, with a rectangular plan divided to serve both military and religious needs.

in spring, dragged on through the following winter. However, some of those set at this time seem to have been the result of fits of rage. The military genius Robert of Bellême mused that a garrison would be scattered in winter simply because no action would be expected, but his subsequent attack on Dangeul in revenge for fortifying the

The earliest representation of a gun, from the manuscript of Walter de Milemete dated 1326. Probably of brass, it fires a large arrow or 'garrot' which may have been made of iron with brass fletchings. In practice the gun would have to be secured to the wooden trestle by ropes. The arrow was fixed inside the barrel by a leather wad attached to the shaft. At this stage such weapons posed more of a threat to persons than property. (Oxford, Christ Church, Ms.92, f.70v)

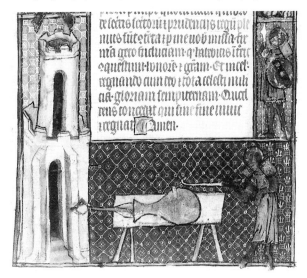

castle (probably in 1098) failed when the news of his intentions reached the garrison. King Stephen, furious that Miles of Beauchamp refused to yield up Bedford castle, likewise attempted a winter assault at Christmas 1137; the garrison was persuaded to surrender 5 weeks later by the Bishop of Winchester.

There were two methods by which a stronghold might be captured—by starving out the defenders, or by assaulting and capturing the fortress. The first method was by far the most economical in lives. Palisades would offer protection to the camp, occasionally set on a rampart to shield the tents of the army. Sometimes ditches were dug in front of the besiegers to guard against sorties, and behind them to guard against attack by relief forces. At Calais Edward III set to work as soon as he arrived in August 1346, erecting houses of planks with straw and brushwood thatch in ordered streets. There was a marketplace, haberdashers and shops selling meat, cloth, bread and other things brought daily by sea from England and Flanders, supplemented by local raids. However, sitting out a siege also had drawbacks. When feudal troops were involved they could only be held in the field for the length of their agreed service, usually 40 days. After this time they were free to leave, and could

An encampment before an Italian city. The Sienese flag flies above the tents. Notice the grass huts. From a fresco of 1328 by Simone Martini. (Palazzo Pubblico, Siena)

only be induced to stay by cash payments. Mercenaries would stay as long as they were paid, but either way the result was expensive for the commander. Similarly in summer there was always the threat of disease such as dysentery, which broke out in the army of Henry V during the siege of Harfleur in 1416, and which the king himself fatally contracted at the siege of Meaux (October 1421–May 1422).

The crusaders faced not only disease but shortage of food and water. The parched countryside around Antioch was soon stripped of food and the crusaders were forced to pay inflated prices for that brought in by Armenians and Syrians. Horses died by the score, and even when the city fell a small loaf sold for a bezant.

When forces were at a premium there might not be enough men to seal off a large stronghold effectively. Some blockades were set by land and sea; at Nicaea in 1097 the crusaders at first had difficulty surrounding the town, but eventually the only egress lay via the lake. The crusaders requested help from the Emperor in Constantinople, who sent ships to Civetot; from there boats were drawn by ox-cart to the lake, filled with Turcopoles, and launched under cover of darkness to seal the city completely. Blockades were not always efficient. When in 1142 Stephen trapped Matilda in Oxford castle during the civil wars his valuable prize escaped one night by sliding down a rope, slipping unnoticed past the pickets amidst shouts and trumpet calls, and fleeing across the snowy countryside in a white cloak.

A tight siege could nevertheless completely reduce a garrison. At such times a castellan might well expel the 'useless mouths', those non-combatants such as villagers who had taken refuge initially. These wretched folk could then only pray that the besiegers acted with decency and allowed them through their lines. The castle well was of major importance; in 1118 Fulk of Anjou entered Alençon only to be confronted by the garrison in the castle. With the help of workmen he found the channel that builders had used from the River Sarthe, and secretly tunnelled underground to cut the water pipes leading to the castle. When water ran out in Exeter in 1136 the garrison used wine to cook and make bread as well as to extinguish fires. During the crusades a well was of paramount

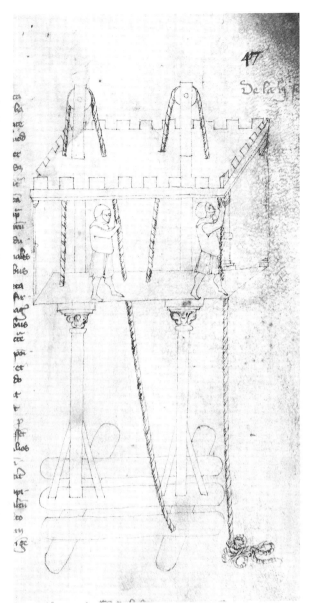

A 14th-century Italian representation of a tower whose platform could be raised by winches worked from inside. From the treatise by Guido da Vigevano. (Bibliothèque Nationale, Paris, Ms. Lat. 11015, f.47v).

importance; at Xerigordon it was outside the defences, and so assiduously guarded that the Christians were reduced to drinking the blood of horses and asses.

The alternative to a truce or total blockade was to erect a siege castle, fill it with men, and then move on with the main army. Sometimes castles could be used to deny provisions and rents to those held by opponents, but at other times small castles were deliberately built close to the enemy gates to

23

counter any movement. They were usually of wood and set behind earthworks. The outline of one such, a motte and bailey siege castle of 1174, survives about 400 yards from the gate of Huntingdon castle. Setting up such a castle could be dangerous. At the second siege of Le Puiset in 1112 Suger remarks that the besiegers suffered from the missiles of the garrison a stone's throw away, despite the beams for the enclosure having been dressed beforehand. Several such castles might be constructed. Sometimes church towers were utilised; Geoffrey Talbot dug up the churchyard opposite Hereford castle to make a rampart and placed siege engines on the bell tower, while at

Antioch the crusaders turned a mosque into a siege-castle and fortified it with tomb slabs.

Raids, sorties and relief forces

A 13th-century French account of an army on the march describes the foremost troops as scouts and incendiaries, followed by foragers. They fired houses and plundered for the army, but there was another reason for their actions. Wasting the land denied provisions to the besieged, destroyed his crops and killed the men who worked his lands. Writing of the attacks on Henry II's fortresses in 1173–4, Jordan Fantosme advocates just this strategy. Simeon of Durham mentions that Henry I wasted for more than 20 miles around Pont-Audemer in 1123. Some commanders car-

A late 14th-century illustration of a city completely surrounded by the tents of the besiegers. (By permission of the British Library)

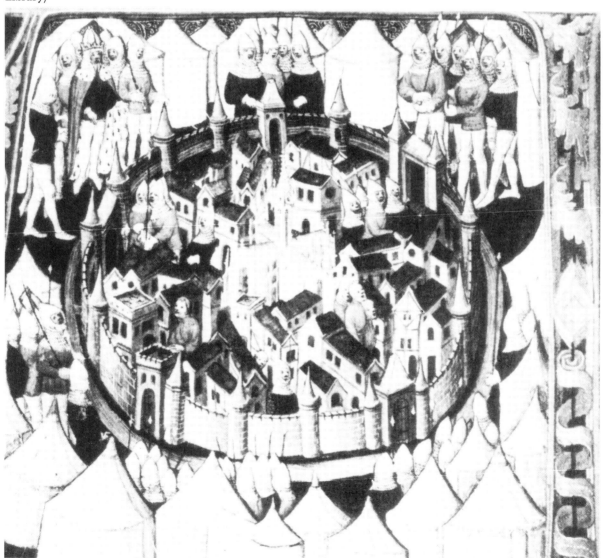

ried out similar actions after failing to capture a stronghold. Thus Orderic Vitalis describes the men of William Rufus as tearing up the vines, cutting fruit trees and smashing fences and walls when rebuffed before Mayet in 1099. The policy of wasting was also designed to tempt out a garrison.

It is a mistake to believe that the defenders of a castle sat inside and waited for the enemy to attack them; this is to misunderstand the rôle of the castle in warfare—it was a fortified base from which armed men could ride out. It follows naturally that, given the opportunity, such warriors would leave their defences to discomfit the enemy. Sometimes this was done before the besiegers even reached their target, men being deployed at river crossings, barriers and forest tracks. In 1119 French raiders on their way to attack Tillières castle were ambushed by the castellan, who had kept the paths patrolled. Sorties were also useful in destroying enemy siege engines and killing men in surprise attacks sometimes launched from sortie passages in the outer walls. The German Emperor Frederick II found himself on the receiving end of one such attack during his siege of Parma in 1247–8. Despite his inadequate forces he built a village called Vittoria outside the city. When he took large numbers of men off on a hunting trip the Italians seized their chance; on 18 February, 1248, they launched a sortie that ended in the killing and capture of several hundred and the sack of Vittoria.

Ransoms might be gained from captured oppo-

An illustration from Konrad Kyeser's 'Bellifortis' of the early 15th century depicting the use of a hooked beam to force down a drawbridge. Also shown are men protected by wattle contraptions rather like bee-skeps. (Niedersächsische Staats-und Universitäts-bibliothek, Göttingen)

Another idea from Konrad Kyeser. The heavy pivoting club is raised by winch, and on release swings down and sends the bolt forward. (Niedersächsische Staats-und Universitäts-bibliothek, Göttingen)

nents, but in addition an element of knightly honour was present in these displays of arms. This is especially seen in the sporting jousts staged to alleviate the boredom between two sides. Sometimes a barrier was erected around the gate to prevent any treachery by the besiegers in hand-to-hand foot combat.

At Courcy in 1091 the Norman garrison fought with Robert of Bellême's men for control of the only oven, which lay outside the walls; Orderic says that in one skirmish 20 were killed. Some commanders insulted their enemies by flinging open the gates and daring them to enter, as happened in 1119 when King Louis of France advanced against the Normans in Breteuil. Sorties, launched for whatever reason, could go dangerously wrong. In 1099 the Norman garrison in Le Mans, having been worsted in open battle with Helias of Maine, fled back to the gates but could not force them shut behind them. In the chaos they lost the town and only just reached the citadel.

Alcázar of Segovia, Spain, a 'great ship' fortress. An 11th-century castle was turned into a royal palace in the early 15th century when Juan II created a 'torre del homenaje' or tower keep. (Courtesy of the Spanish National tourist Office)

Oxford was burned in 1142 when a small group of royalists mingled with the defenders retreating back into the town.

Besiegers faced not only aggressive garrisons, but the threat of relieving forces arriving in rear. The English garrison in Pontoise were relieved four times before it finally fell to the French in 1441. Where siege lines were loose, or besieging forces inadequate (for example in a siege-castle) supplies and men were sometimes brought in unopposed. At other times a prudent withdrawal was made; even William the Conqueror abandoned tents, baggage, arms and furnishings when forced to retire from Dol in 1076 by approaching French and Angevin troops. The siege-castle at Vatteville was stormed during a surprise attack one morning in March 1124. Besiegers were sometimes trapped between the garrison knights and the relieving army, as happened to the Moslem forces before Jaffa. However, when besieging armies were confident of their prowess relief forces faced real problems. Henry V's siege of Meaux in 1422 was so effective that the Dauphin only managed to get one column into the town, after killing the sentries. They climbed the walls on ladders which the garrison had covered in white sheets so that they blended with the walls, but their leader, Guy de Nesle, fell off and was caught by the English as he lay in the ditch. The French forces around Castillon in 1453 set artillery along their lines of circumvallation, which severely mauled Talbot's relief force when it charged their positions. Some clashes precipitated a major confrontation, such as the battles of Tinchebrai (1106) and Lincoln (1141).

Surprise and treachery

Despite formalities in siege warfare, some less straightforward methods were employed to achieve success, such as the use of spies. Beggars in the siege lines around Ballon informed the garrison that Fulk of Anjou's men were at dinner, enabling the defenders to launch a highly successful sortie. In 1364 a monk who carried protection money to La Charité-sur-Loire heard the plan to attack Sancerre, the names of captains and strongholds round La Charité, strengths of contingents and the time they would cross the river. He turned out to be the brother of Guichard Aubergeon, the captain of the garrison of Sancerre, and specially chosen. The attackers were subsequently ambushed and cut to pieces.

Despite the presence of sentries in castle towers there are a number of instances of castles being taken by surprise. There might be a logical explanation; William II seized Mantes in 1097 because the garrison had gone to assess the damage done to the corn and vines the previous day, and were caught as they re-entered. Occasionally a straightforward trick was employed. In 1271 Sultan Baibars forged a letter which ordered the Hospitallers to hand over Krac des Chevaliers. Others were more daring; in 1364 Bascot de Mauléon hid with six others in a haystack near Thurie and next morning, dressed as women, they mingled with those filling pitchers at the spring before walking in with kerchiefs over their faces and blowing their horn for their hidden companions. Similarly in 1401 the Tudor brothers sent a carpenter into Conway who, appearing to arrive for work, slew the two watchmen and seized the castle with 40 others.

Often, however, surprise was the result of treachery. Sometimes this took the form of a simple refusal to respect the code of chivalry, as when the Anjevin count, Geoffrey Martel, was shot in the arm by a crossbowman on the wall as he discussed

A drawbridge designed to collapse under an attacker when a bolt is withdrawn. From Kyeser's 'Bellifortis'. (Niedersächsische Staats-und Universitäts-bibliothek, Göttingen)

One of the most detailed drawings of a trebuchet complete with measurements, from Kyeser's 'Bellifortis'. The pivoting arm has a total length of 18 metres; note the length of the sling. (Niedersächsische Staats-und Universitäts-bibliothek, Göttingen)

peace terms during a parley before Candé in 1106, a wound from which he subsequently died. Often, however, it was the result of a betrayal of one's lord, which to a knight of honour was a particularly base action. The totally ruthless Robert of Bellême used the general confusion following the death of William I to change sides and so capture several castles whose garrisons thought him to be a supporter of the king. Henry I apparently could not support a long siege for fear of treachery, which always dogged conflicts between kinsmen. At Bures he placed Breton and English mercenaries in the castle since he distrusted many Normans. The royal garrison at the fortified manor of the Archbishop's palace at Andely were caught off guard when it was betrayed to the French in 1119; soldiers hiding in the straw in a corn storehouse rushed out in the morning with English warcries, only to change them to French ones once inside, and French cavalry squadrons burst in and seized the town.

Towns to which castles were attached often

presented problems to a castellan, particularly if the castle was seized or built by a conqueror; he was immediately faced with defending the walls of a town whose inhabitants might be as hostile as the enemy without. The Norman Conquest of England forced numerous foreign soldiers on the native population; in York the citizens actually revolted against the garrisons stationed in the two mottes (both of which survive today). The burgesses of both Hereford and Lincoln appealed to King Stephen to come and remove the rebel garrisons in 1138 and 1141 respectively.

Such lukewarm relationships between townsmen and garrison sometimes resulted in disaster for the town. At Le Mans in 1099 the Norman garrison in the castle removed the troops of the claimant Helias by using their catapults to hurl molten dross on to the largely wooden houses. Such extreme behaviour was not especially rare; if occasion demanded, castellans were prepared to destroy their own castles and leave scorched earth behind them rather than see them taken by a superior enemy.

Siege Techniques and Engines

Pyrotechnics

Fire was a particular hazard to a town, for even if its walls were of stone the houses within, huddled close together in narrow streets, were largely of wood and wattle. When Roger of Breteuil attacked Breteuil without warning in 1138 great piles of straw and chaff were lying in front of the houses as a result of the harvest threshing; the town was an inferno in a matter of minutes, and the garrison, taken off guard, were cut down as they fled towards the castle. Even without such unintentional assistance, a besieger could burn down a town in a couple of days, and would do so if necessary; Henry I burned Évreux when he was unable to force an entry into the castle. Neither were castles themselves invulnerable, especially in the 11th and 12th centuries when many were wholly or partially constructed of timber and the domestic ranges in the bailey were usually of wood.

Thus in 1090 Duke Robert of Normandy constructed a smith's furnace before Brionne to allow his archers to shoot arrows with heated tips into the old, dry, wooden shingles of the hall roof. Fire had taken hold before the defenders realised what was happening, a device described as 'ingenious' by the chronicler Orderic Vitalis.

A conventional fire-arrow was simply made by winding tow impregnated with pitch round the shaft and igniting it. Larger versions could be made to shoot from ballistas, though firebrands or flaming wooden arrows might be substituted. Hand-held firebrands consisted of wooden batons whose ends were probably soaked in fat, pitch or some other combustible. Barrels or terracotta or glass pots (which would shatter on impact and spread the contents) were filled with flaming pitch, tar or animal fat; the small ones could be thrown by hand, the larger by catapult. Some writers even

A cannon in action, with crossbows shooting fire-arrows, from a German manuscript firework book of about 1440. (by courtesy of the Board of Trustees, Royal Armouries)

advocated sending animals with burning ropes attached into towns via sewers or crevices.

The defenders similarly sent combustibles against besiegers and their engines. At Mayet the defenders used burning coals in vessels to destroy piles of wood used to fill the ditch and props for the foundation of a causeway to the palisade.

One inflammable product widely feared was Greek Fire. It was probably evolved by the Byzantines in the 7th century, and is likely to have reached Europe via contact with the Crusaders. Early instances of its use in the West come from the sieges of Montreuil-Bellay in 1151 and Nottingham in 1194. The 'Book of Fires for the Burning of Enemies', compiled under the name of Marcus Graecus in c.1280 and probably Byzantine in origin, provides the earliest Western reference to the ingredients of Greek Fire, these consisting of live sulphur, tartar, sarcocolla and pitch, boiled salt, petroleum oil and common oil, boiled and soaked into tow before being ignited. There were probably several versions in use, based on liquid, paste and solid mixtures. Burning liquid was also shot from tubes with a kind of pump, and could be used on land in a sort of syringe. Used in conjunction, paste was likely to stick to a target, while powder could be lit before release to provide the fuse. It could be thrown in vessels like other combustibles. Marcus Graecus also provides a version of Greek Fire in which a distillate was soaked into paper wicks put into a square arrow pierced with holes, ignited and shot from bows or ballistas.

Greek Fire appears to have been difficult to

Ideas for war machines, from sketches in the manuscript of Walter de Milemete, dated 1326.
(1) A type of kite carrying incendiary materials, which are flown over a town and released. (2) A rare drawing of a catapult worked by the torsion of twisted ropes. Most illustrations show trebuchets, and though crude and partially inaccurate this sketch is based on a practical machine. (3) A machine for throwing Greek fire. The manuscript also shows a similar device for throwing bee skeps into a castle!

extinguish, water proving useless on its own. The 12th-century chronicler Geoffrey de Vinsauf, as well as noting the stench, believed that only vinegar could quench it, and that sand could only lessen its ferocity. Though not widely used in the West it was greatly respected. The Moslems in Acre hurled jars of the stuff at the Frankish belfreys and other structures near the walls and burned everything. The French Crusader Joinville vividly describes the roar it made, and the fiery tail, a tall spear's length, which it left as it flew through the air when launched from the Saracen catapults during the 5th Crusade in 1250. Thomas of Walsingham recalls its use together with other missiles by the French defenders of Ypres in 1383, which caused the English to flee their guns.

To counter the danger from combustibles both defenders and attackers might place freshly flayed hides over exposed timbers where possible. The 'Mappae clavicula de efficiendo auro' (probably originally of the 8th century) suggests layers of leather, felt and wool impregnated with fermented urine or 'vinigar' (a word which also covered other acidic solutions), although in practice leather, turf, manure, French chalk or clay might rather be pressed into service, or timber might be soaked with some solution which left a skin on the surface.

Sand, ash or earth was used to smother fires. When stone and brick castles became common besiegers aimed at the wooden hoardings, or the timber domestic buildings within; 15th-century treatises are full of machines for bringing fire to a fortress.

Noxious gases are occasionally encountered. At the siege of Beaucaire during the Albigensian 'Crusade' in France the defenders let down a sack containing sulphur, tow and glowing embers; the combustion caused the sulphur to give off choking fumes, which drove off the besiegers at the foot of the wall. In the early 15th century Konrad Kyeser noted the properties of burning sulphur, pitch, resin and horses' hooves. Alexander Borgia, the pope, was accused in 1498 by a Basque captain of the king of France of using asphyxiating gases at Ostie.

Escalade

The most hazardous method of taking a strong-hold was by direct assault. This meant either climbing over the walls or penetrating via a breach made by sappers, miners, rams or artillery.

The cheapest method in materials, but the most hazardous to life, was that which involved using ladders to climb the walls. Scaling ladders were often simple wooden affairs, perhaps with iron hooks at the top to grip the parapet and sometimes with iron points at the base to dig into the earth; some were secured by wedges. Other types were occasionally used; the 'Gesta Stephani' mentions ladders made of thongs for a night attack on Devizes in 1140 by Robert FitzHubert. Some 15th-century treatises show ladders made of straps and buckles, examples which extended like a

The great bombard, 'Mons Meg', now held in Edinburgh Castle. Made from longditudinal iron strips strengthened by additional bands, it now rests on a replica carriage. On site the gun originally was strapped down to a wooden bed, tiller or trunk. Recent research has shown that the breech did not unscrew as previously thought, and the function of the slots remain something of a mystery. Forged in Belgium in 1449 and sent to Scotland eight years later, the bombard weighs 6,040 kilos and has a 48 cm. calibre. It left Edinburgh to besiege Norham in 1497 to the accompaniment of minstrels and promptly broke down in the city suburbs despite the presence of five carpenters and 100 workmen. Erich Egg has estimated that it could hurl a stone ball of 150 kilos perhaps 263 metres. (Historic Buildings and Monuments, Scotland).

hinged trellis, or heavier wheeled versions. Not all proved serviceable; during the 1st Crusade both at Antioch and Ma'arrat al Numan the Frankish ladders broke under the weight of armed men. At the siege of Rome by Arnulf's Germans in 896 a heap of packs was used to scale the wall.

As the besiegers advanced they would be met with a hail of missiles. At times, more especially in the later period, they might advance along trenches dug under cover of a bombardment. Their first task was to negotiate the ditch or moat, the former sometimes filled either with stakes to slow the advance and thus create easier targets, or small iron caltrops to cripple the attacker. Occasionally they might use portable wooden bridges. Once at the wall base, the besiegers would try to erect their ladders and ascend. They presented targets for rocks, scalding water or wine, hot sand (which entered crevices in the armour) and fire pots. (Boiling oil, so beloved of Hollywood, is mentioned only occasionally.) Forked poles, used to help erect the ladders, were also used by the defenders to push them away before they could hook over the battlements. Pole weapons fitted with hooks could also be used. Several assault teams might simultaneously attack two or three chosen sections of wall to spread out the defenders' resources or divert their attention. During an assault the besiegers were given covering fire by their own archers, slingers and crossbowmen, themselves protected by wooden pavises or else by large shields called mantlets. These were usually of wood, often set on wheels, and were also used to cover the entrance to a penthouse or to protect a siege engine.

Further assistance might be provided by a 'belfry', *beffroi*, or siege tower. Some assaults succeeded without additional effort; at Ma'arrat a tower was built only after the ladders had failed, since a belfry was a huge and costly structure. Such wooden towers had to be high enough to overtop the wall. The occupants of the upper storey could see everything going on in the castle; Roger of Wendover relates how, at the siege of Bedford in 1224, Henry III's belfry was so effective that no man of the garrison dared to remove his armour in case he was shot dead. They could also sweep the parapet clear of defenders prior to an assault, hence they were sometimes dubbed *malvoisin* or 'bad neighbour'. At the siege of Lisbon in 1147 it is reported that two towers, 95 and 83 feet high, were constructed.

A tower was divided up into several floors (*coenacula* or *solaria*) connected by ladders, and might be fitted with loopholes in the timber walls for archers and crossbowmen. These towers were propelled on wheels or rollers, either by men inside using crowbars to lever the wheels round or by

Methods of reaching the wall top.
(1) An engine for making swift attacks by raiding parties, from Guido da Vigevano, 14th century. (2) A wheeled scaling ladder and winch, from Valturio, 1472. (3) Valturio's design for an engine like that of Guido.

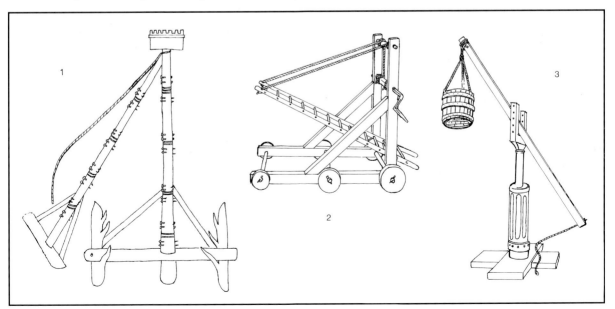

In this drawing from the book 'De Machinis' of *c.* 1449, by the Italian Mariano di Jacopo detto Taccola, mines have been dug beneath a stronghold, but instead of combustibles gunpowder is being used to destroy the props and bring down the wall. He advises that when footsteps are heard overhead, a vault is constructed with 3 or 4 barrels of powder in it which could be left open at the top. A sulphur-soaked rope is then laid into a barrel and a thick wall of stones, sand and lime built at the doorway before the rope is lit. Below can be seen movable penthouses.

oxen. The latter might be fastened to traces running through pulleys fixed to stakes, so that as they pulled away from the castle the belfry moved towards it. Once the tower was in position the wheels could be removed. Belfrys were often fitted with a movable drawbridge which could be dropped on to the battlements to allow storming parties to rush across and capture a wall top. The lowest storey might carry a penthouse roof jutting out at the front to protect sappers at work at the wall base, or a battering ram might be slung under it. A siege tower was made as late as 1645 by the royalists during the English Civil War.

Such towers became prime targets as they slowly approached. They were usually covered in raw hides to protect them against fire, the greatest danger; Richard I even used plates of iron on his towers at Acre. At Dyrrachium (1108) and Damietta (1169) the defenders built their own tower inside the wall to counter that of the besiegers. The defenders at Dyrrachium in 1081 also built a tower, and using mechanisms and manpower pushed a beam from it to jam shut the drawbridge of the Frankish belfry. The Moslems in Tyre in 1111 destroyed a large Frankish siege tower by erecting on a mast a horizontal beam complete with iron-sheathed tip. They then proceeded to use a system of pulleys to winch out buckets of flaming oil, tar and wood shavings. Sometimes the defenders prepared the ground in front of a wall by digging pits and refilling them with soft earth, in the hope that if a siege tower was brought up it would sink into a pit and be rendered useless.

In order to bring such a tower or any siege engine close up to the wall the ditch or moat had to be filled at the required point. This meant tipping masses of earth, turf, stones, wood and fascines into the gap to form a solid surface that might then be planked over. This was carried out under enemy fire, and often movable penthouses were constructed to cover the work, sheds on wheels made of wood and covered in the hides of mule, calf or ox or occasionally iron plates. The men under them would fill the ditch slowly, advancing the penthouse as they did so. Men enjoyed giving names to their siege engines, so a penthouse was called a 'cat' or a *vinea*. Another name was the 'sow', perhaps because some had humped backs covered in hide and occupants who tore at the earth, or perhaps because the men working below them were huddled together like piglets. At the siege of Dunbar by Edward III an English penthouse under which men were working on the walls was crushed by a stone; as the soldiers scurried away the Scots 'Black Agnes' shouted that 'the English sow has farrowed'.

Sap and mine

When faced with wooden palisades a besieger could try to set them on fire, shatter them with catapults or else hack a way through with axes, as happened at Le Puiset in 1111. One of the most effective ways to breach a stone wall was to undermine the foundations and cause a section to collapse. The simplest method was to attack the

Siege of Jerusalem, 1099 (see text commentary for detailed caption to all colour plates)

A

B

C

Seaborne attack on Acre, 1189

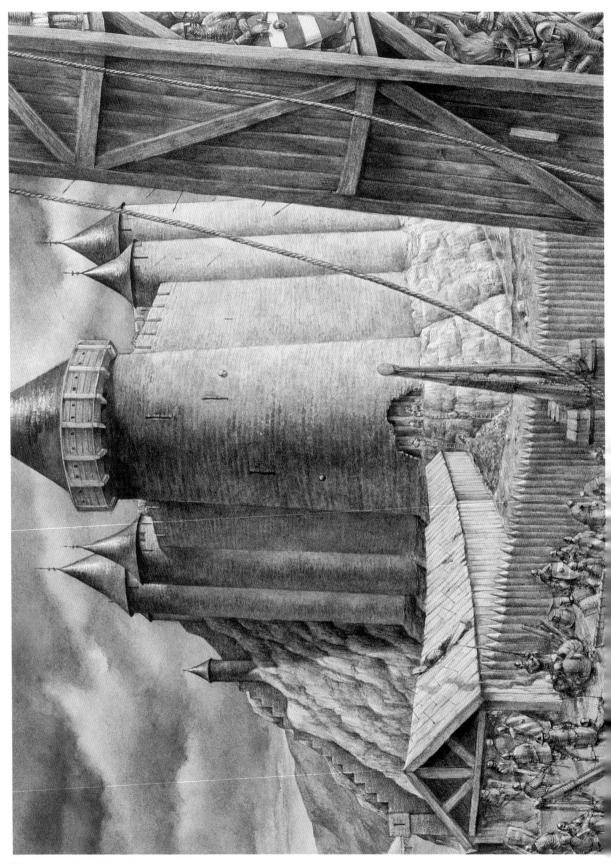

D

Battering ram, mid-15th C

E

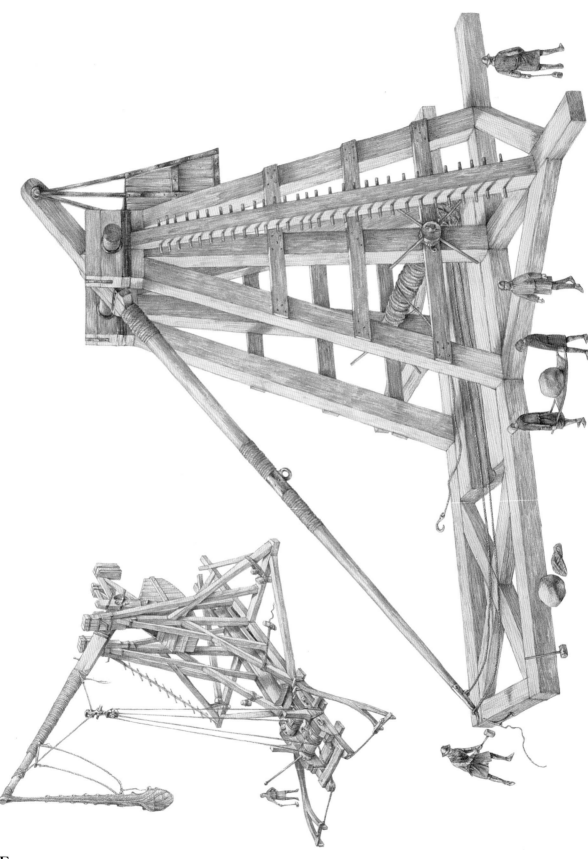

F

Ballista, c.1330

3

4

Siege, later 14th C

5

6

2

1

H

Bombard, siege of Orleans, 1429:
1: Master gunner
2: Shield bearer
3: Gunner
4: Assistant gunners

Castle defenders, c.1480:
1: Handgunner
2: Collineator
3: Petardier
4,5: Crossbowmen

J

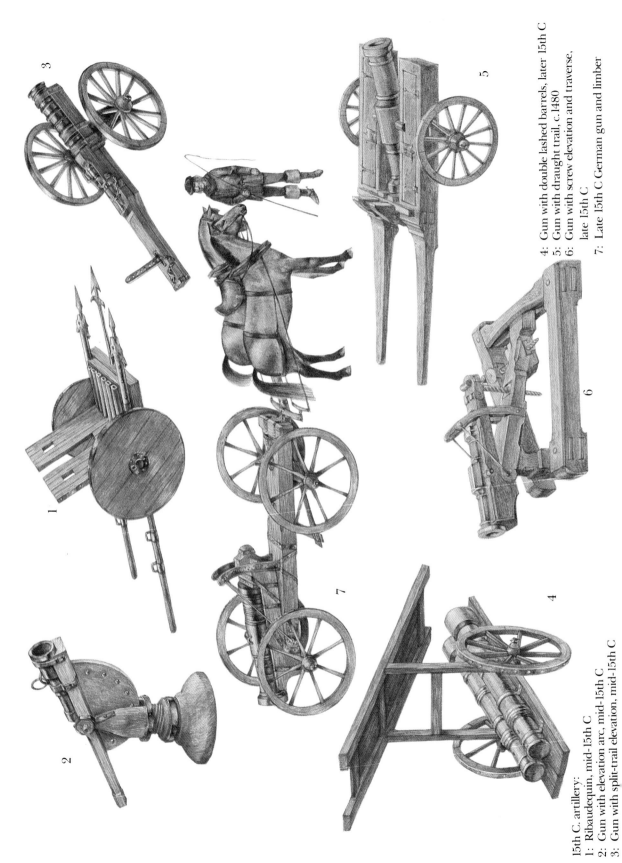

15th C. artillery:
1: Ribaudequin, mid-15th C
2: Gun with elevation arc, mid-15th C
3: Gun with split-trail elevation, mid-15th C
4: Gun with double lashed barrels, later 15th C
5: Gun with draught trail, c.1480
6: Gun with screw elevation and traverse, late 15th C
7: Late 15th C German gun and limber

K

base with picks, the sappers being protected by movable sheds or a trench roofed with planks; the cavity could then be shored with timbers and filled with combustibles, and when fired the props would burn through and collapse, bringing down a section of the wall above. Occasionally sappers worked unprotected, as at Acre in 1191, where the cash incentives offered by Richard I seem to be the only explanation for such rash behaviour.

The mine was perhaps the most lethal weapon in the besieger's store; builders tried where possible to site their castles on solid rock, or else to provide them with a wet moat, both of which would deter miners. Where such a site was lacking, the wall base was sometimes splayed in order to thicken it. More rarely a curtain wall was provided with relieving arches along its length so that, should part of the wall be breached, the arch would prevent the whole section collapsing.

Ideally a mine was started at a distance from the walls and shielded from sight by sheds or hurdles to ensure that the defenders did not realise what was happening. If houses were present these could be used to conceal the mine opening. As the mine progressed the roof was shored with timbers. Once under the foundations of the wall, a gallery was excavated, all the while using props to shore up the work. When complete, the cavity was filled with combustibles and the mine fired. From the early 15th century barrels of gunpowder might be used instead, and from about mid-century zig-zag passages were designed to protect against blast. In a Sienese manuscript of c.1470 there is a reference to the use of a compass by the miners.

Occasionally a mine was driven past the wall so that during the night a party of besiegers could come up inside the castle perimeter and open the

The sap and the mine:
(1) A trench is dug to the base of the wall, and under cover of wooden planks the stones are removed and the gap shored with timber, ready to be fired. (2) A mine is driven under the wall and the gap shored with timbers. The entrance is concealed wherever possible, and the shaft slopes down from the wall in case the defenders flood it. (3) A mine comes up inside the enciente, the final layers being removed by night to allow a raiding party to enter the castle. (4) A countermine attempts to break into the mineshaft.

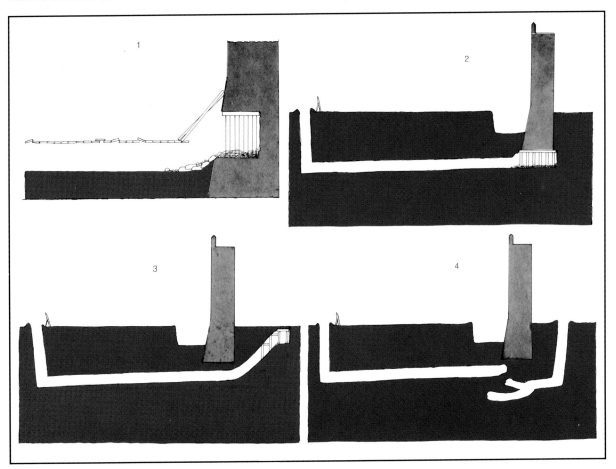

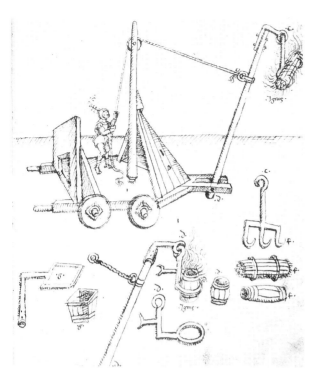

One of Taccola's many designs for taking fire to a fortress. The arm can be lowered from behind the wooden mantlet (Taccolo says such protective shields must always be used) and several interchangeable holders are illustrated for barrels or fascines.

Coca castle, a mid-15th-century Spanish concentric castle with tower keep, is famous for its 'mudéjar' brickwork. (Courtesy of Spanish National Tourist Office).

gates. Prudent garrison commanders might place bowls of water on a wallwalk or on the ground, so that any disturbances underneath would register as ripples on the surface. Sometimes a desperate attempt was made to plug the breach, as happened at Dover in 1216 when a section of the northern gatehouse, brought down by French miners, was filled with timber by Hubert de Burgh's men, who subsequently beat off the French. Two other alternatives are illustrated by the siege of Carcassone in 1240; the defenders built several palisades and a dry stone wall inside their defences to oppose the mines, which they heard being dug beneath them. They also dug countermines to break into the enemy workings. Locating a mine was not always easy, and the countermine might itself further weaken the walls, but when a breakthrough occurred ferocious hand-to-hand fighting would take place underground. An attempt by the Franks to mine Dyrrachium (1108) was frustrated when the Greeks broke in and blew Greek Fire through reed pipes into the faces of the enemy miners. Some countermines were dug as a precaution to siege; at Coucy a spring at ground level in the countermine could be utilised to flood a mine once a vertical shaft was dug into it.

Mines were so dangerous that it was sometimes

unnecessary to fire the workings. When in the 14th century Lord Burghersh secretly drove a mine under the tower of the castle at Cormicy in France he invited the knight in charge of the castle to visit the work. The mere sight of the excavation caused the well-provisioned French to offer an immediate surrender.

Ram and bore

Another method of breaching the wall involved the use of the bore and battering ram. The bore consisted of a wooden beam fitted with a pointed iron tip, which was pushed against the masonry and turned by handles or a bow until the head had bored a hole into the wall. Its action earned it the name of 'musculus', for it gnawed away like a mouse. The bore was particularly aimed at sharp angles. The battering ram consisted of an enormous tree trunk repeatedly swung against the same piece of wall until it dislodged and cracked the masonry; equally it could be used to smash down a door. The ram was usually furnished with an iron head (at Acre this took the form of a giant mill-stone axle) and slung from a framework of stout beams. Sometimes up to 60 men were employed to rhythmically swing the huge beam, unlike the bore which only needed a few hands to turn it. Both ram and bore would normally be concealed within a wooden penthouse. Sometimes the ram was dubbed *testudo* because its form was like that of a tortoise with its head moving in and out of its shell. Some late medieval illustrations portray rams consisting of a wedge-shaped shed shod at the pointed end with iron and set on wheels.

Artillery

The study of medieval pre-gunpowder artillery is beset by problems. The word 'artillery' itself was first used to cover all types of war gear. Descriptions of engines are frequently not lucid enough nor illustrations accurate enough to allow detailed reconstructions to be made. To complicate matters, medieval authors used numerous names for such engines and are not consistent in so doing.

Thus we find 'petrarie' used as a general term for stone-throwing engines, as well as 'mangon', 'trebuchet', 'robinet', 'mate-griffon', 'bricolle', 'beugle', 'bible', 'matafunda', 'malvoisin', 'war wolf' and 'engin a verge'. Some of these terms were also applied to belfrys. It may be that this love of nicknames suggests that such machines were not abundant; conversely the lack of mechanical description may suggest they were so common that they normally aroused little excitement.

Before the introduction of cannon, artillery pieces could be divided into three categories: those which worked by tension, by torsion, and by counterpoise. Artillery utilising tension included the *ballista*, which took the form of a giant crossbow in which propulsion was provided by a large horizontal bow. Although such weapons could probably be adapted to shoot stones from a pouch in the centre of the bowstring, they usually shot large wooden arrows or bolts, furnished with iron

A 'goat' or 'chèvre' was used to transfer heavy guns from their carriages on to their tillers in order to be fired. This drawing is from a 1472 edition of Valturio.

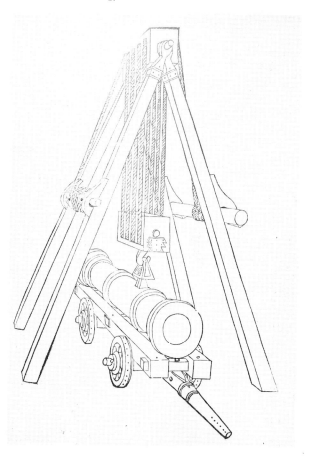

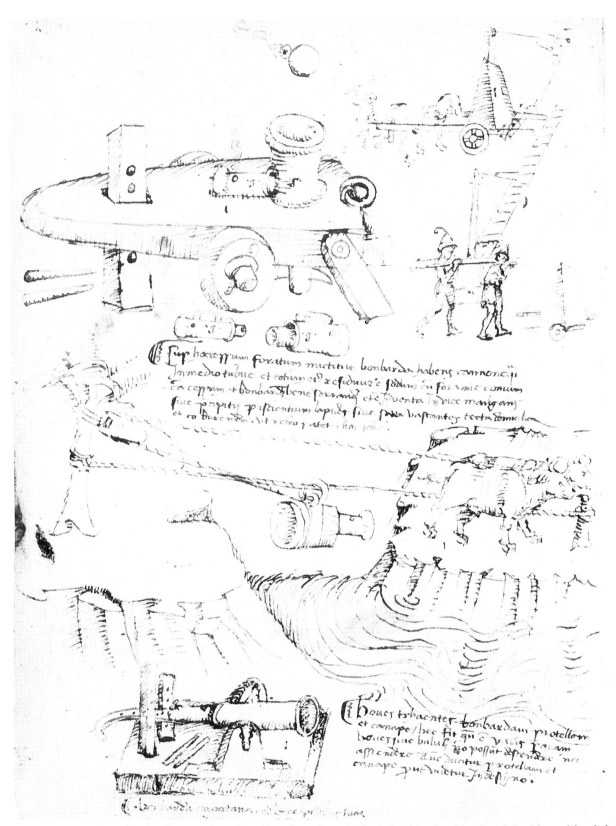

A method of hauling a bombard over a river, from Taccola. Above may be seen a mortar set in a thick carriage with a pierced post and pegs for adjusting the aim. It has a separate breech block fixed in the side, though in this position it is highly unlikely to have worked. Next to it are ideas for pivoting ladders or bridges.

heads and often fletched with wood or brass. They were so powerful that they could penetrate several individuals at one shot, as at the Viking siege of Paris in 885–6 when the sight of several Danes skewered together caused Abbot Ebolus to suggest they be taken to the kitchen like so many fowls on a spit. The ballista was better adapted for use in the defence of a castle since stone walls could not be penetrated by the bolts, and in addition it required less space to operate than a catapult. Some versions of the ballista may have followed Roman practice in utilising torsion, whereby each half of the bow was separate and thrust through a vertical skein of rope or hair twisted by ratchet and lever until the bow arm was forced forward. With a bowstring attached, any attempt to bend the bow automatically strained the two arms against the skeins.

It is this torsion method which was used in the earliest type of catapult, sometimes called the 'mangon', or 'mangonel' (the latter possibly a smaller derivative). Here the skein was set horizontally and a stout beam inserted into the middle before twisting the skein and so forcing the beam up vertically against a padded crossbar. The end of the beam was furnished with a cup (rather than the more efficient sling used by the Romans), and the whole forced down with a winch.

The third type of engine was that worked by counterpoise. This version, the 'trebuchet', was the only style not derived from Roman and Greek prototypes. The Arabs probably adopted it by the end of the 7th century, and it appeared in the West in the early 12th century. In 1147 these weapons seem to have been used by the crusaders at the siege of Lisbon. This early form was the traction trebuchet, also sometimes confusingly styled as the 'mangonel'. Basically the machine consisted of a long beam (or set of beams bound together) pivoted between a pair of uprights. Ropes were attached to one end of the beam and a sling to the other. A stone was placed in the sling and a group of men hauled on the ropes and so pivoted up the longer end of the beam. At the critical moment the sling opened and released its missile. More detailed accounts come from Arabic and Chinese writers; according to the latter, teams of men varied from 40 to 250 or more. Murda b.'Ali mentions Arab, Persian or Turkish, and Byzantine or Frankish models, which differed in points of detail.

The counterweight trebuchet, which appeared in the Mediterranean in the late 12th century, worked on the same principle except that a box filled with earth, sand, stones or lead was substituted for the muscle power of men (it has been estimated that it weighed between 10,000 and 30,000 lbs.). The sling was much longer, and when loaded was contained in a trough below the engine. Aegidio Colonna at the end of the 13th century describes several varieties of counterweight machine: the 'trabuchium' had a fixed counterweight box; the 'biffa' had a counterweight that rotated around the beam, giving greater range but less accuracy than the former. Its exact form is not known, but Donald Hill has pointed out that if one type simply had a fixed box and the other a slung box as often shown, the result would be the same; the 'biffa' thus remains unknown. The third variety was the 'tripantium', which had both a fixed and rotating counterweight.

The amount of timber needed for such machines was enormous; at Damietta in 1249 St. Louis captured 24 engines whose timber could provide stockade material for the whole camp. Edward I employed 50 carpenters and five foremen to build the 'war-wolf' which was transported to the siege

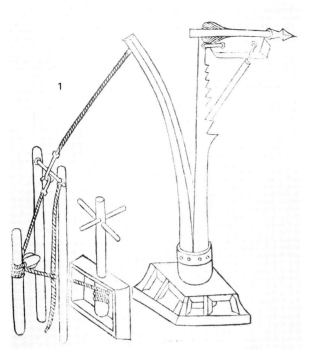

Designs for spring engines: (1) The beam is winched back, the hook released by the transverse bar and the impact of the beam discharges the missile. The angle of flight can be adjusted by way of the pivoting arrow-rest; from the 1453 edition of Valturio. (2) Utilising a supple length of wood, this version is adapted to throw two stones; from the late 15th-century 'Il Codice Atlantico' of Leonardo da Vinci. (Biblioteca Ambrosiana, Milan)

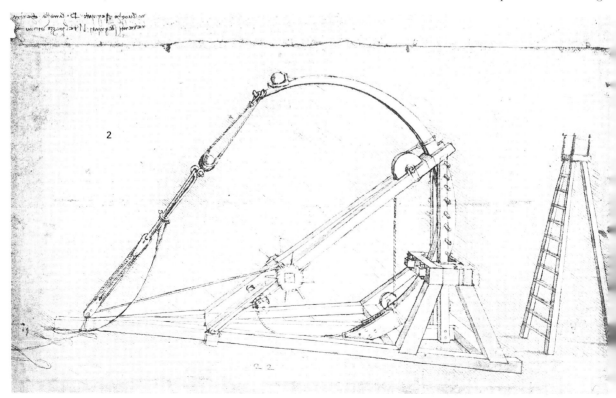

of Stirling by land and water. The king was so proud of his machine that he refused to accept the Scots' surrender until he had struck the walls with it. In 1421 the Dauphin Charles paid his master of works in the Touraine 160 *livres tournois* for one large 'coyllar' or trebuchet that could shoot a stone of 400 lbs. and another that used 300 lb. balls. Occasionally smaller, wheeled versions (perhaps those called 'bibles') were seen. The first mention of a 'trebuchetarius' or maker of trebuchets appears by 1228; while in 1244 one such in Northumberland had stones cut from a form and mould, suggesting a standardisation of weapons.

It is difficult to be anything like precise when speaking of the size of missiles and the ranges of catapults. Some large machines shot enormous stones (in 1188 at Sahyun in the Holy Land balls weighing up to 600 lbs. were used). Otto of Freising notes that in 1155 a stone shot during the siege of Tortona fragmented against a wall and killed three knights taking part in a council by the cathedral door. Unlike the mangon, the trebuchet lobbed its missiles in a high trajectory, and on average its stone balls were about 100–200 lbs. in weight and could probably be hurled about 300 yards. Sometimes such care was taken in selection of ammunition for catapults that it was transported for miles; for one large petraria at the siege of Newcastle Emlyn in 1287, 480 stones were collected from the shore below Cardigan and transported by boat and then by 120 packhorses and carts.

Froissart says that during the siege of Mortagne by the Count of Hainault in 1340 an engineer made a machine to oppose one of the besieger's engines, and broke its arm with the third shot. The rate of fire apparently could be surprisingly fast; 'De Expugnatione Lyxbonensi' asserts that at Lisbon in 1147 two engines worked by relays of men shot about 5,000 stones at a rate of one stone every 15 seconds. During the siege of Kenilworth

French soldiers fill a ditch with fascines and boards under the direction of Joan of Arc, here shown in a rather fanciful helmet. From a miniature of the second half of the 15th century. (Bibliothèque Nationale, Paris)

in 1266 Henry III employed nine catapults day and night; both sides shot so vigorously that stones were colliding in mid-air. During some large-scale sieges many machines were used; at Acre in 1191 a Moslem writer asserts that 300 catapults and ballistas were employed by the Crusaders. A crude version of germ warfare was also employed; in 1422 Prince Coribut, employed by the Grand Duke of Lithuania, is said to have had the bodies of men slain by the defenders shot into Carolstein together with 2,000 cartloads of manure, which apparently resulted in the spread of infection.

Even during the later years of the 15th century catapults could prove effective despite the improvement in cannon. During the siege of Burgos in Spain (1475–6) trebuchets and bombards were both used, whilst at Rhodes in 1480 a Christian catapult caused great damage to the siege lines despite the Turkish use of guns.

Cannon

The words 'gun' and 'gunner' may derive from the mangon served by its 'gynours'. The earliest reference to a gun is in a Florentine ordinance of 1326, which mentions a brass cannon, arrows and iron balls. Later chroniclers refer to cannon at the

siege of Metz in 1324. The first known picture of a gun is that illustrated in the manuscript of Walter de Milemete of c.1326, in which a vase-shaped weapon set on a trestle shoots a dart—hence the names 'vasi' and 'pots de fer' for early cannon. The name 'bombard' ('bombos'—a loud hum) is not seen until the mid-14th century, and at that time denoted several sizes of weapon. However, by the end of the century it had come to denote the larger siege guns.

The earliest guns were made of copper or brass, but after about 1370 cannon began to be made of iron longitudinal strips or iron sheets forged into tubes and with hoops heat-shrunk over them. This method of manufacture became increasingly common, especially for large cannon. Removable breech chambers containing the powder were introduced for some guns, being fitted into the breech with leather-covered wedges. However, as they leaked powder-gas muzzle-loaders gained in popularity. Guns were mounted on wooden tillers with thongs, ropes, wire or iron bands, though the tillers appear to have needed replacing every few days. By the mid-14th century wheeled 'ribaudequins' were in use, consisting of a number of small barrels mounted on a tiller with a wooden shield for the gunners, and perhaps originally made to guard gates, etc. Heavier guns utilising wheels were probably uncommon in the West until the mid-15th century. Elevating carriages appeared in about 1400, and trunnions became general in the second half of the century. In the 15th century there were enough types of gun for different categories to arise, enabling a table of approximate sizes to be produced.

Bombards could weigh up to 10,000 lbs. and could hurl a stone ball up to 7 cwt. The next size was the 'veuglaire' or 'fowler', about eight feet in length, from 300 to (rarely) several thousand pounds, often breech-loading. The 'crappaudine' was smaller, from four to eight feet long, whilst the often long-barrelled culverines and serpentines were the smallest. A mid-15th-century source directs that when the bombard has been discharged the veuglaires and other lighter pieces should keep up rapid fire to stop the defenders from

Greek fire is dropped from pots on to ship-borne attackers. From a manuscript of the second half of the 15th century. (By permission of the British Library)

The assault on Ribodane, from a manuscript of c.1475. Missiles are shot from the top of a wooden siege tower, which is provided with pivoting covers. (By permission of the British Library)

making repairs. Mortars appeared towards the end of the 14th century, the English having 15 breech-loaders at the siege of Orleans in 1428. At first short and with a wide bore, they became smaller in the 15th century. By the closing years cast bronze guns were superseding the welded and hooped iron examples.

The earliest guns fired small balls, or bolts called 'garrots', usually made of oak and fitted with iron heads and fletchings of iron, steel or brass. They weighed on average 15–30 lbs., but allegedly could reach 200 lbs. These remained common until c.1340 and were in use throughout the Middle Ages (for example at the siege of Ardres in 1377, and for use in culverines by Charles the Bold of Burgundy in the 15th century). Lead pellets for small guns and iron balls were gradually replaced by gun stones, the first reference being in the chronicles of Pisa in 1364. These were carefully cut, and could be covered in lead to prevent wear to the barrel. In 1451 the accounts of Philip the Good of Burgundy refer to stones of 900 lbs. The danger from gunpowder was illustrated in 1460 when a hooped bombard called 'The Lion' exploded at the siege of Roxburgh and killed James II of Scotland.

A Burgundian manuscript of the 1470s notes that a bombard requires 24 horses to draw it, a crappaude eight, a serpentine or mortar four, and

53

The fate of many strongholds once they were seized is shown in this illustration from the second half of the 15th century. (Bibliothèque Nationale, Paris Ms. Français 2644, f. 135)

a small serpentine two. In 1477 two Italian bombards required 48 wagons each with two or four horses to transport the tillers, gunpowder, shot and equipment. Bridges and roads sometimes needed reinforcement, and large guns were often taken by river as an easier alternative. This proved a disadvantage for the Teutonic Knights, who found that the Lithuanians could utilise the strong current to get their siege artillery up-river faster than the Germans could haul theirs into Lithu-

ania. By 1500, however, batteries of 30 or 40 pieces could be brought and set up in front of a town within a day, according to a Florentine observer of French practice, after which they could keep up continuous fire day and night. At such times several thousand rounds could be fired over a few days, though the guns were not always effective, and if only 30 paces from the moat were vulnerable to counter-attack.

The decline of the castle

It has often been said that gunpowder sounded the death knell for the castle, but this is only partly true. Cannon had been used effectively from an early period; they were used with trebuchets to capture the Teutonic Knights' fortress of Marienwerder in 1386. On occasion the mere appearance of heavy guns was enough to cause capitulation; in 1451 the English in Bayonne held out against the lesser guns until the French commander Dunois brought his bombards into action. However, this is not the whole story. Though Henry V effectively bombarded Harfleur into submission (helped by sappers) in 1415, it was starvation, not cannon, which prompted Rouen to yield four years later.

The response to the trebuchet in the 12th century had been to heighten walls against the greater trajectory of the weapon. The introduction of gunpowder prompted some response from castle builders, but this was slow. Loopholes cut to accommodate guns and walls designed to withstand cannon fire were by no means universally adopted. Though gunports were provided at Carisbrooke on the Isle of Wight as early as 1380, these were often designed for hand weapons. Builders tried lower, thicker walls with steep scarps to deflect shot, yet not until the later 15th century

was any real move made towards constructing effective defences against siege guns. Italy was the cradle of the new design—low, massive bastions with gun platforms, and casemates designed to enfilade the ditch with shot. Such arrangements placed military importance first, and domestic arrangements suffered. By the time of the Tudor gun forts in the 16th century cannon had been around for about 200 years.

Changing lifestyles, whereby lords did not wish to live under conditions of military hardship, together with more settled times in some countries, assisted the move away from massive defences. In Scotland, where attack by armed companies was still likely, tower houses continued to be built, but were designed to frustrate local raids rather than full-scale sieges, and built with an eye for comfort. The castle, largely replaced by the fort with its gun platforms, had outlived its usefulness in a changing society.

Further reading:

Anderson, William, *Castles of Europe* (1984)
Brown, R. Allen, *English Castles* (1976)
Brown R. Allen (ed.), *Castles, A History and Guide* (1980)
Contamine, Philip, *War in the Middle Ages* (1984)
Finó, J. F., 'Le Feu et ses Usages Militaires', in *Gladius*, IX, 1970, pp. 15–30
Finó, J. F., 'Machines de Jet Médiévales', in *Gladius*, X, 1972, pp. 25–43
Heath, Ian, *Armies of the Middle Ages*, 2 vols (1982, 1984)
Hill, Donald R., 'Trebuchets', in *Viator*, 1973, Vol. 4, pp. 99–116
Smail, R. C., *Crusading Warfare, 1097–1193* (1972)
Toy, Sidney, *Castles, Their Construction and History* (1985)
Warner, Philip, *Sieges of the Middle Ages* (1968)

The Plates

Burgundian troops lay siege to Morat in 1476, from Diebold Schilling's 'Amtliche Chronicle' of *c.*1480. A bombard pokes out from its protective mantlet, whilst in the foreground a wheel-mounted piece is provided with a pivoted cover. On the march the latter could lay along the brass barrel to guard against rain. The chest contains powder charges held in bags. (Bibliothèque de la Bourgeoisie de Berne, Mss. h. h. I. 3)

A: The siege of Jerusalem, 1099
This plate depicts the moment when knights of the 1st Crusade succeeded in setting foot on the walls of Jerusalem in August 1099. The siege had begun on 7 June, and although they broke through the

outer wall on the northern side they had insufficient ladders and were forced to withdraw.

Two Genoese galleys and four other ships arrived at Jaffa on the 17th with food, as well as ropes, nails and bolts for siege engines; but wood was scarce, and not until the Franks reached the forests round Samaria, 50 miles north, was enough obtained for engines. Raymond of Toulouse and Godfrey of Bouillon began constructing siege towers fitted with catapults and covered with ox and camel hides. Not expecting these formidable objects, the Moslems hastily fortified the walls. Godfrey had one siege tower and machine transported round to the east and reassembled, since this area was a weak spot. The crusaders took three days and nights to fill the ditches to allow the towers to cross; the 'Gesta Francorum' relates how a penny was offered to any man throwing three stones into the pit. Meanwhile the Moslem and Frankish catapults hurled stones and inflammables at one another.

A late 15th-century German design for a catapult worked by two steel springs, which are tensed as the arm (also of steel) is brought down. It has a sling to take a second missile.

By the evening of 14 July, Raymond's tower was across the outer defences and over the ditch on the side of Mount Sion, to be followed by Godfrey's the next morning at the north-east wall close to the present Gate of Flowers. A smaller tower was to make a feint attack against the north-west angle. Resistance was spirited, and the towers were racked by the stones, tar, pitch and other burning stuffs flung against them. Sacks of cotton and hay, carpets and timber beams had been hung over the walls to absorb the Frankish bombardment. At about midday, while Godfrey's men strove to drive off the Moslems on the walls, the crusaders cut down two of the beams and pushed them out from the siege tower across to the wall top where they formed a foundation for the bridge when it was lowered. Then they set fire to the sacking. Smoke billowed up and forced the defenders to virtually abandon a section of wall. The bridge came down and Godfrey and his men rushed across; ladders were hastily erected to give extra support. The Gate of the Column was opened and the knights in the other siege tower also succeeded in storming across. There followed a massacre which con-

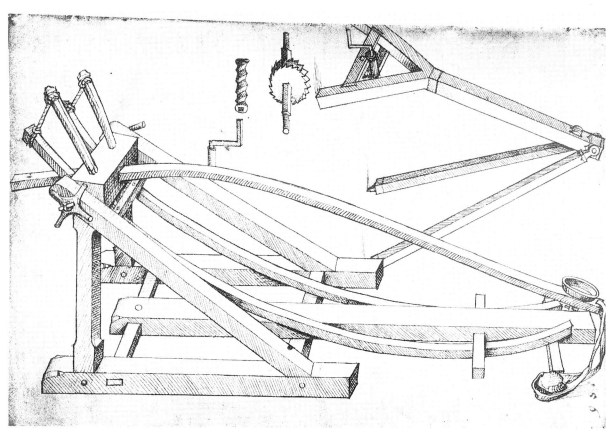

Caltrops were iron spikes scattered before fortifications to lame attackers and their horses. They were so designed that one point was always uppermost. In this late 15th-century Swiss illustration caltrops are being dropped during an assault. (By courtesy of the Board of Trustees, Royal Armouries)

trasted poorly with the Moslem treatment of captured cities.

B: The first siege of Le Puiset, 1111

Le Puiset was a motte-and-bailey castle in the Beauce in northern France whose earthworks survive today. Louis VI decided to attack the place to stop its lord, Hugh de Puiset, from taking dues from the surrounding area. Louis attacked the gate with carts full of wood smeared with pig fat and coagulated blood with which he hoped to burn them down. Vigorously resisted, the attackers were reduced to protecting themselves with planks and anything else that came to hand. The attack was beaten off, as was a simultaneous attack on the palisades which was broken up by a mounted sortie. Finally a party of men cut through the palisades with axes and Hugh surrendered. The timber tower on the motte was burned down on the king's orders, though it was rebuilt and subsequently besieged again.

C: The sea-borne attack on Acre, 1189

Whilst the Western armies of the 3rd Crusade approached Acre, King Guy of Jerusalem settled down to besiege it. One of the first assaults was carried out by the Pisans using their ships. A large tower covered in hides was constructed on the ships and, supported by other vessels fitted with catapults, was manoeuvred up to the Tower of Flies, which stood at the end of a promontory at the harbour mouth. After a fierce struggle, during

which Moslem ships vied with those of the Crusaders, the defenders succeeded in throwing Greek Fire on to the siege tower and setting it and the other machines alight. We have reconstructed the tower resting on a platform across two galleys of a type believed to have been used during this period in Mediterranean areas.

The siege was continued on the landward side, especially when Philip II of France and then Richard I of England arrived. The fleet blockaded the sea approaches and earthworks stretched round the city from shore to shore. Surrender terms demanding release with life and property were rejected. Three siege towers were built, protected from missiles by thick twists of rope hung in front, and two of Philip's huge machines were named 'God's Own Sling' and 'The Wicked Neighbour'. Moslem catapults destroyed several Christian machines, assaults were thwarted because every time the Crusaders advanced, the relief forces of Saladin attacked the camp and

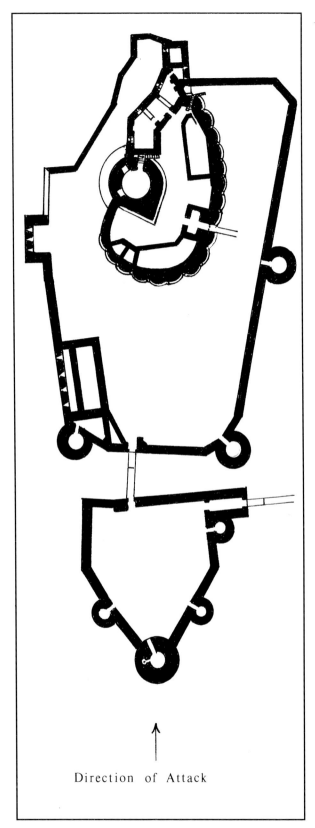

Direction of Attack

Chatêau-Gaillard, showing the only direction from which Philip could attack the castle.

increased pressure for their return to defend it. A mine dug beneath one tower was foiled by a countermine. After much damage and loss of life the Moslems finally submitted, and were greatly admired for their courage.

D: The siege of Château-Gaillard, 1203–4

When John took the English throne in 1199 he found himself faced by the wily Philip II of France. The latter decided to advance against Château-Gaillard, which stood on the Norman borders on a rock outcrop between two rivers. Philip took the little town of Les Petit Andeleys at the foot of the castle, and beat off a relief force. He then dug two lines of trenches from one river to the other, setting wooden towers at intervals between the lines. Many townspeople had taken refuge in the castle, and as supplies dwindled Roger de Lacy, who held it, began expelling 'useless mouths'—the old, the sick, women and children. The first thousand were allowed through the French lines, but the next crowd were refused. During the bitter winter of 1203–4 they clung to life in the ditches round the castle until Philip came up to examine the scene and ordered the survivors to be fed. Many died, unable to digest the food.

In spring Philip decided to attack. The only direction of advance was a spur near the outer ward. Here he brought up a siege tower, catapults and mantlets. His sappers pushed a penthouse out and began filling the ditch, but the work was so slow that they clambered down ladders to the ditch and thence up the slope to the foot of a large tower where they excavated a hole and fired the props to bring it down. The French stormed across, only to be confronted by the walls of the middle ward.

Against the curtain on the south side was a chapel with latrines beneath. A French soldier found the drain outlet, climbed the shaft and emerged below the window. On a companion's shoulders he reached the window and pulled others up by rope; they then created havoc to terrify the garrison into believing a large force was inside. The defenders fired the building and fled to the inner ward while the French lowered the drawbridge for their own troops. Now a mine was dug under the inner wall; a countermine broke in, but this weakened the masonry and a catapult broke up the wall. The defenders in the inner ward fought as long as they could but were overwhelmed. As they did not use the keep it has been suggested that the battlements may not have been completed.

E: Battering ram, mid-13th century

Battering rams are amongst the oldest recorded forms of siege engine. They consisted of a huge tree trunk shod with iron and protected by a stout penthouse of timber covered by fresh hides against fire. A rhythmical swing was set up by gangs of men sheltering under the penthouse. A ditch would first have to be filled and perhaps planked over to allow the ram across. Here the wheels are shown chocked to steady the machine; in some cases they were taken off altogether. Thick mattresses were lowered by defenders to cushion the impacts, and forked poles might be used to catch and hold the head. The iron grapple shown here comes from a manuscript of about 1300. A grapple used by Moslem defenders at Tyre in 1111 pulled the ram sideways so fiercely that the shed was nearly toppled over. During the attack on Beaucaire in Provence during the Albigensian 'Crusade' of the first half of the 13th century a noose attached to the arm of a machine was lowered to catch the ram's head.

F: The trebuchet, later 13th century

The only medieval catapult not based on classical predecessors was the trebuchet, which appears in manuscripts practically to the exclusion of other types. The counterweight trebuchet shown here is based on several manuscript illustrations; when the counterweight drops the sling on the other end is pivoted into the air. Very long slings are frequently illustrated in contemporary manuscripts, and would be essential for optimum performance. As in a number of miniatures, the arm is here shown released by a hammer blow, though others show a rope used to pull off the iron triphook. It is not known for certain how these machines reacted, since models cannot be used to gauge the performance of a full-sized machine. Such large machines were nearly always constructed on site and may occasionally have been prefabricated.

The smaller picture shows the famous illus-

Carrier pigeons were occasionally used to transmit messages during a siege. From a late 15th-century German woodcut.

tration by the 19th-century antiquary Viollet-le-Duc. The ground frame is based on the mid-13th-century sketch by Villard de Honnecourt. The two curved wooden pieces near the winches appear to be springs, which, when tensed by one windlass and then released, served to pull the arm of the catapult down slightly from the vertical before winching it back in the conventional manner. Other points to note on his reconstruction are shock absorbers sticking out in front of the counterweight; the sling terminals both tied on so the sling does not come open; the release pin at the top of the winch rope; and his idea that one cord represents a drag when fixed from the arm to the sling, so lessening the range by a given amount depending on the area of the sling to which it was fastened. An early 15th-century illustration shows the release rope hooked over a peg, which could be fitted into a series of holes bored in the side of the ground frame, thus adjusting the range.

G: A ballista, c.1330s

These essentially anti-personnel weapons are rare in medieval art. This reconstruction is based on illustrations in the Walter de Milemete manuscript and the 'Romance of Alexander'. The ballista is essentially a large crossbow with a stout wooden stave. The centre channel slides forward to engage the string, and is drawn back by the use of a screw and winch; equally a winch and pulley could be used. Pulling back the lever allows the claw to pivot back and release the missile. Several illustrations simply show a solid table construction with no wheels and no means of elevation. The large wooden 'garrots' were fletched wood or with brass and carried four-sided iron heads. By *c.* 1300 the ballista was also called a 'springald', a name occasionally applied to another engine (see Plate H2).

H: A siege in the later 14th century

We have attempted to show here a number of machines and techniques that might be employed

Portable bridges for crossing ditches or moats.
(1) An extending wooden platform, from Kyeser, *c.*1405. (2) A bridge floating on barrels, from Kyeser. (3) A penthouse with drawbridge containing a smaller 'cat' with flammables on the end of a pole, from Taccola, *c.*1449. (4) A bridge which can be unfolded, from Valturio, 1453.

in a siege before gunpowder was widespread. A number of items come from 'Bellifortis' by Konrad Kyeser at the turn of the 15th century, and were copied during the century. Similar ideas are repeated in late 15th-century manuscripts.

H1: Catapults utilising the principle of torsion are rarely illustrated. This comes from a 15th-century manuscript and so was probably a fairly rare item in an age of trebuchets and early guns; nevertheless, it is a workmanlike piece. The arm does not project too far above the crossbar, otherwise it might break with the impact. The torsion on the skein can be increased with a ratchet.

H2: A spring engine; a few illustrations allow such machines to be tentatively reconstructed, though again many are rather later in date. The angle of aim can be altered by the support rod below the javelin head, and the whole rotates on a stand. The spring action of the wooden bar sends the javelin flying from what was an anti-personnel weapon.

H3: A machine to place a group of men swiftly

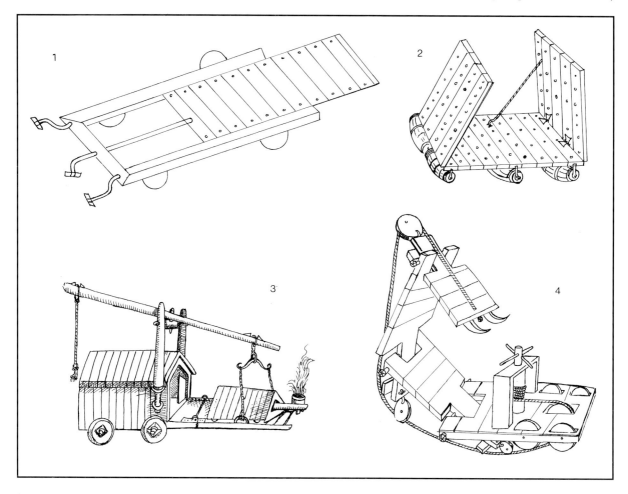

behind the battlements. The operators, assisted by the weighted arm, work within the wooden engine. We must wonder about the efficacy of such machines, since by their very nature they telegraphed where an attack was due, and the number of attackers was very limited. Some illustrations do not even show wheels or protective covering.

H4: The ditch has been filled but the mobile shed has been disabled. Approaching the barbican is a 'castle-cat' or 'chat-chastel', so called because it combines a small tower and shed. This one incorporates a battering ram, and such a machine was dubbed a 'crane'. Some large machines might be drawn by oxen and utilise pulleys, though a simple winch system might be substituted for draught animals, or even men with levers inside the engine itself.

H5: A 'crow' in action. Victims could be used for interrogation or ransom, depending on their status. Though occasionally mentioned in chronicles, contemporary illustrations are scarce.

H6: Part of the curtain wall has been damaged by mining, but the defenders, aware of the mine's existence, have managed hastily to construct a wooden palisade behind the breach. The attackers, protected by pavises and mantlets, and by the covering fire of archers, have driven posts into the ground to act as pivots for a timber frame covered with hurdles and dropped like a drawbridge. Undaunted by the new defences, they try to raise their ladders, one of which is pushed away by a fork.

H7: Mantlets of various shapes and sizes were used by archers, crossbowmen and observers. Most were made of wood, but wicker and even iron versions are illustrated in manuscripts.

Dead animals, offal or manure were sometimes hurled into strongholds to encourage disease. This woodcut of *c.*1507 by Kölderer shows a dead horse loaded into the sling of a trebuchet.

I: Bombard at the siege of Orleans, 1428–1429

The Earl of Salisbury besieged Orleans and sealed off the city by 12 October, 1428. He was killed 12 days later; his replacement, Suffolk, waited for the main Anglo-Burgundian forces to arrive in December before pressing the siege. By April 1429 the Burgundians had quit the siege, leaving insufficient troops to surround the city and man the string of redoubts or 'bastilles'. Joan of Arc arrived from the north on 27 April and was slipped in ahead of her soldiers, while barges attempted to float supplies down the Loire. Adverse winds foiled this move but carts were brought overland instead. Exploiting the weakness of English forces on the eastern side, French troops (with Joan) sallied out on 4 May to seize the Bastille de St. Loup, and two days later crossed to the south bank of the river to take those of St. Jean le Blanc and Les Augustins.

On 7 May Joan attacked Les Tourelles, a stronghold controlled by Sir William Glasdale which straddled the bridge connecting the city with the south bank. The English in the hornwork on the south bank failed to reach those in Les Tourelles, itself under attack in rear by the garrison, who had repaired the bridge. Though wounded by a crossbow bolt Joan inspired her troops and caused Les Tourelles to surrender, a move which persuaded the English to abandon the siege the following day.

Bombards such as this one were built to hurl large balls at walls. According to the 'Journal du Siège' the English fired 124 stone balls from bombards and cannon on 17 October alone. The barrel of this example is based on that in the Historisches Museum in Basel. It is 271 cm. long with a bore of 34 cm. Unmixed powder was carried in barrels of sulphur, saltpetre and charcoal; when ready-mixed the contents often separated out during transport. Corned powder was discovered late in the 15th century; this was moistened with alcohol and water and formed into cakes, which could be broken into crumbs. It was also less affected by damp, but, being powerful, was only safe to use in handguns and cast brass cannon.

II: Unarmoured master gunners ('artillatores')

The siege of Orleans, 1428–9, showing the bastilles of the Anglo-Burgundian forces.

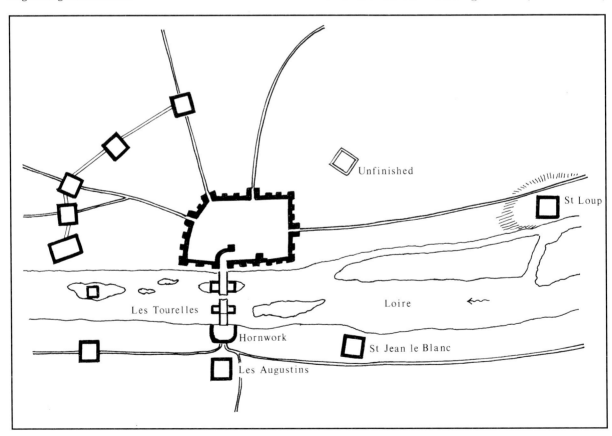

were in charge of gun-casting and, as here, might tour their emplacements laying the pieces. The Earl of Salisbury had four such men in his forces.

I2: A shield bearer escorts the master gunner to protect him against missiles. He carries a light but strong pavise of wood and leather and wears a padded gambeson. His head is covered by a Montauban helmet, a type of kettle hat with a broad brim useful for deflecting missiles in siege operations.

I3: Gunners are usually depicted as unarmoured. A slow match or red-hot wire was used to touch off the powder. It is rare in contemporary illustrations to find even four men in charge of a gun.

I4: Artillerymen or assistants were necessary to haul up pivoting shields which protected the crew until the moment of firing. They also had to swab the barrel clean of hot detritus, ladle in and ram home the powder, and load the ball, here weighing about 1 cwt.

J: Defenders on a parapet, c.1480

Notice the holes of the machicolations through which offensive materials could be dropped.

J1: A handgunner with a 'hook gun' ('Hackenbusch', anglicised to 'Hackbut') designed so that the projection on the barrel presses against a wall to absorb recoil. Some had an iron rod forged in one piece to form a stock. Serpentine levers and triggers were also used in matchlock versions.

J2: A second man (the 'collineator') was often employed to assist in the firing of these larger handguns. He touches off the powder with a slow-match. Illustrations rarely show the ramrod in position under the barrel.

J3: 'Petardiers' threw earthenware pots to shatter in the faces of their enemies. Such pots were filled with pitch or other combustibles and fitted with slow-matches. This petardier wears a brigandine and an Italian barbute helmet covered in velvet.

J4: The powerful crossbow was well suited to defensive positions where the weapon could be reloaded in relative safety. Here the weapons are fitted with steel arms which are bent by means of a windlass.

J5: An assistant reloads a second bow to speed up the rate of fire. Two men might similarly occupy an embrasure in a wall.

K: Gunpowder artillery

Cannon multiplied in design and shape as the 15th century wore on. This selection of guns shows the variety in use. Some pieces were used both for siege and field work.

K1: A 'ribaudequin' or organ gun of the mid-15th century, consisting of several small barrels mounted in a row. Fitted with breech powder chambers, such anti-personnel weapons were useful in defending gates and passageways.

K2: Mid-15th-century gun elevated by inserting a pin through the pierced arc at the required point.

K3: Mid-15th-century cannon raised by a split trail. This breech-loader had an iron powder chamber, which fits into the breech and is secured by a wooden wedge slotted through behind it.

K4: A pair of barrels lashed to a frame and provided with a wooden canopy, from a manuscript of the second half of the 15th century.

K5: A cannon of about 1480 in which the trails double as shafts for a draught horse or horses in tandem, while the sides of the carriage are designed to act as containers with hinged lids. By this date iron trunnions attached to the barrel were becoming popular as a means of elevation.

K6: A cannon of the late 15th century in which vertical and lateral elevation is carried out by means of screws.

K7: A German gun of the late 15th century mounted on its limber. The trail pivots round a spike on top of the limber.

A Scène représentant le 15 juillet 1099 alors que la tour de siège de Godefroi de Bouillon était lancée contre la muraille nord-est de Jérusalem. Les Croisés se servirent de deux poutres (qui avaient été placées à l'origine sur les murs par les défenseurs de la ville, avec des sacs et matelas, pour absorber le bombardement des catapultes, mais qui furent coupées et prises par les assaillants); celles-ci servent de base au pont pivotant monté sur la tour d'assaut. Ils mirent feu à la bourre, et après que la fumée ait forcé les défenseurs á reculer de cette section de perapet, les Croisés abaissèrent le pont et se précipitèrent à l'assaut.

B Louis VI de France échoua tout d'abord lors de son attaque contre le Baron Hughes de Puiset qui lui avait désobéi; sa tentative en poussant des chariots enflammables emplis de brindilles conre la porte de ce château à motte et à douves échoua sous une pluie de projectiles. Le château fut pris par la suite

A Das Bild am 15. Juli 1099, als der Belagerungsturm von Gottfried von Bouillon gegen die Nordost-Mauer Jerusalems vorrückte. Die Kreuzfahrer benutzten zwei Balken (ursprünglich von den Verteidigern der Stadt zusammen mit Säcken und Matratzen auf den Mauerrand gelegt, um den Katapultbeschuß abzufangen, dann aber von den Angreifern erbeutet) als Basis für eine Shwenkbrücke auf dem Belagerungsturm. Die Belagerer steckten das brennbare Material in Brand, und als die Verteidiger durch den Rauch von dieser Stelle der Mauerkrone zurückge-triben wurden, senkten die Kreuzfahre die Schwenkbrücke auf die Mauer und stürmten darüber in die Stadt.

B Ludwig VI. von Frankreich erlebte zuerst einen Fehlschlag bei seinem Angriff gegen das Schloß seines autständischen Barons Hugues de Puiset; der Versuch, mit Karren Feuerholz vor das Burgtor zu bringen, wurde mit einem Hagel von

lorsqu'une section des palissades furent coupées à la hâche, et la tour en bois, sur le tertre en terre, fut brûlée sur l'ordre du Roi. (Elle fut recontruie à une date postérieure, et assaillie une nouvelle fois).

C Reconstitution possible de l'attaque par Gui de Lusignen qui uilise une tour de siège montée sur des bateaux pisans et manœuvrée jusqu'à la Tour de Flies. La tour à bord du bateau dut brûlée plus tard par les défenseurs en utilisant un "feu grec".

D Tour d'assaut, catapultes et mantelets protègent les troupes de Philippe II de France alors qu'elles s'approchent d'une tour par une longue tour d'assaut pour creuser un trou dans les fondations de cette première; les étais furent ensuite brûlées, et la tour s'effondra, mais un mur intérieur arrêta j'assaut suivant. Le château tomba finalement, mais seulement après qu'un seul soldat se soit faufilé à travers le fût de la chapelle, pour ouvrir une brèche à ses camarades.

E Un pont de fortune a été construit sur le fossé pour permettre à la tour bélière sur roues de s'approcher de la muraille. Des peaux de bêtes fraiches servent à la protéger contre le feu. Les défenseurs ont abaissé un large coussin pour amortir l'impact du bélier, et une fronde avec laquelle ils essaiaient d'en attraper la tête pour la soulever; l'on utilisa également des harpons pour attraper et renverser les béliers.

F Cette large illustration est établie d'après plusieurs images de manuscript des grands trébuchets de "contrepoids"; l'on voit souvent de très longues frondes, qui seraient nécessaires au succès de l'opération. La plus petite version est établie d'après la reconstitution de Viollet-le-Duc à partir d'un croquis du 13ème siècle par Villard de Honnecourt. Il montre des amortisseurs en face du contrepoids; les deux extrémités de la fronde sont nouées, afin qu'elle ne s'ouvre pas pendant l'opération; et une corde part de l'articulation de la fronde, sa position réglant sa portée.

G Fondamentalement une arme antipersonnel, on ne les trouve que rarement sur les illustrations des manuscripts du Moyen-Âge. L'eflût central à rainures glisse vers l'avant pour engager la fronde, et est ensuite réenroulé avec le treuil. Le levler de détente enclenche la corde. Les illustrations semblent présenter un cadre solide, mais la hausse ou la course verticale ne sont pas prévues.

H Une gamme de machines de siège, prélevées principalement sur le manuscript de Bellifortis du début du 15ème siècle. **H1** Catapulte à torsion – rare dans les manuscripts d'époque. **H2** Lance-javelot à ressort, pivotant sur un appui et corde d'élévation. **H3** Grue à contrepoids pour soulever une partie des assaillants et leur faire franchir les murailles – l'on peut s'étonner de l'efficacité d'un dispositif aussi visible. **H4** "Chat-castel" comprenant une petite tour et une tour équipée d'un bélier. **H5** "Corbeau", mentionné de temps à autre dans les chroniques – une grue pour empoigner un prisonnier. De nouveau, il fallait, l'on peut imaginer, un certain effet de surprise. **H6** Une partie de la muraille s'est effondrée, après avoir creusé sous les fondations, mais les défenseurs ont construit une palissade intérieure. L'on a fait pivoter un pont temporaire sur le fossé, et les assaillants essaiaient de poser des échelles, que les défenseurs repoussent à l'aide de longues fourches. **H7** Des mantelets en bois, en osier tressé, et même en fer servaient à protéger les assaillants.

I La bombarde, décrite d'après un exemple qui a survécu à Bâle, d'un calibre de 34 cm et tirant des balles de pierres. La poudre tendait, à cette époque, à se séparer, lorsqu'on la transportait déjà mélangée; c'est pourquoi des barils de soufre, de salpêtre et de charbon étaient amenés jusqu'aux positions du canon. **I1** Maître-canonier, un civil spécialiste, recevant un salaire très élevé. **I2** Un soldat portant un casque "Montauban" au bord large (chapel de fer) protège le canonier avec un pavois en bois et cuir. **I3** Les canoniers sont généralement représentés sans armure; ils tiraient leur canon avec une mèche brûlante ou un fer rouge; **I4** Des aides tenaient le bouclier pivotant qui protège le canon jusqu'au moment du tir. Ils devaient également écouvillonner le baril, charger la poudre en vrac et des balles de 45 kg.

J1 Canonier avec Hackenbusch. **J2** Collineator, second canonier, tirant le canon avec une mèche lente. **J3** Des pétardiers lancent des pots remplis de combustible et porant des amorces à mèche lente. **J4, 5** Il fallait du temps pour charger les puissantes arbalètes avec des barres d'acier, elles convenaient donc bien à un emploi défensif sur un parapet protégé.

K L'on vit au 15ème siècle une large variété de canons: **K1** "Canon-orgues" – chaque affût a sa chambre à poudre à la culasse. Utile pour la défense des portes, etc., contre les assauts d'infanterie. **K2** Canon pointé en haut, en insérant une goupille dans les trous d'un arc perché. **K3** notez la piste fendue et pivotante qui permet de rehausser la pointe du canon; et la chambre à poudre enclavée dans la culasse. **K4** Un manuscript de la fin du 15ème siècle présente ce canon dont les affûts sont amarrés à un cadre sous un dais. **K5** Canon datant de 1480 environ, avec piste fendue pour former des traits servant à atteler un cheval; coneneurs aux couvercles articulés sur les flancs du chariot; et tourillons pour hausser la pointe. **K6** Canon avec vis pour régler la hausse et la course verticale. **K7** Canon allemand avec avant-train.

Geschossen vereitelt. Das aus Holz und Steinen erbaute Scholß wurde später erobert, also man einen Teil der Palisaden mit Äxten zerstörte. Der hölzerne Burgturm wurde auf Befehl Ludwigs niedergebrannt. (Die Burg wurde später wieder aufgebaut und nochmals belagert.)

C Eine mögliche Rekonstruktion des Angriffs von Guy von Jerusalem, unter Verwendung eines Belagerungsturms, der auf Schiffen aus Pisa ruhend bis an den Turm der Fliegen heranmanövriert wurde. Der Turm wurde später von den Verteidigern mit griechischem Feuer zerstört.

D Der Belagerungsturm, Katapulte und hölzerne Schutzschilde schützen die Truppen König Philips II. von Frankreich, als sie sich einem Turm durch eine langen Schutzgang nähern und ein Loch an der Turmbasis graben; die Hilfsmittel wurden danach angezündet, und der Turm fiel, aber einen innere Mauer hielt den nach-folgenden Angriff auf. Die Burg wurde schließlich nur dadurch eingenommen, daß ein einzelner Soldat durch den Latrinenschaft der Kapelle ins Burginnere kroch und den Eingang für seine Kameraden öffnete.

E Über den Graben wurde eine provisorische Brücke geschlagen, um dem Rammblock, der sich in einem auf Rädern laufenden Schutzgang befand, die Annäherung an die Mauer zu ermöglichen. Die Verteidiger ließen eine große Matte herunter, um den Anprall des Rammblocks zu dämpfen, sowie auch eine Schlinge, mit der sie den Rammbalken zu fangen und anzuheben versuchen. Für das Einfangen und Umstürzen von Rammbalken wurden auch Haken an Seilen verwendet.

F Die große Abbildung beruht auf mehreren in Manuskripten gefundenen Bildern großer Steinschleudermaschinen mit Gegengewichten; manchmal sieht man sehr lange Schlingen, wie sie für gute Leistung dieser Maschinen erforderlich waren. Die kleinere Version beruht auf der von Viollet-le-Duc vorgenommenen Rekonstruktion einer Zeichnung aus der Mitte des 13. Jahrhunderts von Villard de Honnecourt. Hier sieht man Stoßdämpfer vor dem gegengewicht; beide Enden der Schlinge sind verknotet, damit sie sich bei Verwendung nicht öffnet; ein Seil läuft vom Arm der Maschine zur Schlinge – damit wurde die Reichweite des Wurfes verändert.

G Im Grunde eine Waffe gegen feindliche Soldaten; man findet sie nur selten in mittelalterlichen Manuskript-Illustrationen. Der mittlere gerillte Tragbalken wird vorgeschoben, um die Schnur einzuspannen, und wird dann mit der Winde zu-rückgezogen. Der Auslösehebel löst die Schnur aus. Abbildungen scheinen einen festen Rahmen zu zeigen, ohne Vorrichtungen für Richtungsänderungen.

H Eine Reihe von Belagerungsmaschinen, meistens dem Bellifortis-Manuskript aus dem frühen 15. Jahrhundert entnommen. **H1** Spannkatapult, selten in damaligen Manuskripten. **H2** Speerwerfer mit Federung, auf einem Ständer rotierbar; Wurf-winkel durch eine Stange veränderlich. **H3** Gegengewichtskran, mit dem eine Gruppe von Angreifern auf die Burgmauer gehoben wird – die Wirksamkeit eines so offen erkennbaren Gerätes scheint fraglich zu sein. **H4** Die "Burgkatze", mit einem kleinen Turm, einem Schutzgang und einem Rammbalken. **H5** "Krähe", manchmal in historischen Aufzeichnungen erwähnt – ein Kran für das Anheben eines Gefangenen. Auch hier fragt man sich, wie unaufmerksam ein Soldat sein müßte, um davon gefangen zu werden. **H6** Stollen haben einen teil der Mauer zum Einsturz gebracht, aber die Verteidiger haben eine innere Mauer aufgerichtet. Eine Hilfs-brücke wurde über den Graben geschlagen, und die Angreifer versuchen, Leitern anzulegen, die von den Verteidigern mit langen Gabeln weggestoßen werden. **H7** Schutzschilde aus Holz, Rohrgeflecht oder sogar aus Eisen wurden zum Schutz der Angreifer verwendet.

I Die Bombarde – beruhend auf einem erhalten gebliebenen Stück in Basel – hat ein Kaliber von 34 cm und versendete Steinkugeln. Schießpulver schien zu jenen Zeiten beim Transport in fertig gemischter Form zu zerfallen, weshalb man separate Läufe mit Schwefel, Salpeter und Holzkohle zu den Geschützstellungen brachte. **I2** Ein Soldat mit einem breitkrempigen "Montauban"-Helm (Chapel de fer) beschützt den Kanonier mit einer Pavese. **I3** Kanoniere werden meist unbewaffnet gezeigt; sie zündeten ihre Kanonen mit glosenden Scheiten oder glühenden Drähten. **I4** Helfer richten den Schild auf, der die Kanone bis zum Augenblick des Feuers schützt. Sie mußten auch den Laut reinigen, loses Pulver einschütten und die 50 kg schweren Steinkugeln laden.

J1 Kanonier mit Hackenbusch. **J2** Der Collineator, der zweite Kanonier, zündet die Kanone mit einem glosendem Holzstück. **J4, 5** Starke Armrüste mit Stahlstäben benötigteo lange Zeit zum Laden, waren also sehr für Verteidigungskampf auf geschützten Mauerkronen geeignet

K Im 15. Jahrhundert gab es es gab es eine große Vielfalt von Kanonen: **K1** Die "Orgelkanone" – jeder Lauf besaß seine eigene Hinterlader-Pulverkammer. Gut geeigner für die Verteidigung von Toren usw. gegen Infanterieangriffe. **K2** Kanone wird angehoben mittels eines durchbrochenen Bogens, in die je nach Wunsch Bolzen gesteckt wurden. **K3** Drehschiene ermöglicht Anheban der Kanone; separate Pulverkammer. **K4** Ein manuskript aus dem späten 15. Jahrhunderts zeigt diese Kanone in einem Rahmen gebunden Läufen, geschützt von einem Dach. **K5** KaNone etwa aus dem jare 1480, mit einer Spaltlafette, in die ein Pferd eingespannt werden kann, und mit Schildzapfen zum Anheben, **K6** Kanone mit Schrauben zur Regulierung des Schußwinkels. **K7** Deutsche Kanone mit Protze.